Joseph Reeve

Miscellaneous Poetry

In English and Latin

Joseph Reeve

Miscellaneous Poetry
In English and Latin

ISBN/EAN: 9783337777852

Printed in Europe, USA, Canada, Australia, Japan

Cover: Foto ©Thomas Meinert / pixelio.de

More available books at **www.hansebooks.com**

MISCELLANEOUS POETRY,

I N

ENGLISH AND *LATIN.*

SECOND EDITION.

By the Rev. JOSEPH REEVE.

Exeter

PRINTED BY R. TREWMAN AND SON.
SOLD BY THEM AND J. ROBSON AND CO. NEW BOND-
STREET, LONDON.

1794.

UGBROOKE PARK.

A

POEM.

THE RIGHT HONOURABLE

CHARLES LORD CLIFFORD,

BARON OF CHUDLEIGH, &c. &c.

THIS POEM

IS RESPECTFULLY INSCRIBED

BY HIS LORDSHIP's

MOST OBEDIENT HUMBLE SERVANT,

THE AUTHOR.

PREFACE.

THE noble family of the Cliffords of Chudleigh, by the male line, is defcended from Sir
Lewis Clifford, the third fon of Roger, Baron
de Clifford, whofe Grandfather was made a
Peer by King Edward I. in the year 1300.
The family has been fince honoured by the cre-
ation of a fecond Peerage in the perfon of Sir
Thomas Clifford, the ninth in defcent from Sir
Lewis. Sir Thomas Clifford received this
honour from King Charles II. under the ftile
and title of Lord Clifford, Baron of Chudleigh,
by letters patent dated April 22, 1672. In
November following he was made Lord High
Treafurer of England. This Nobleman's
Grandfather Thomas Clifford, D. D. was the
firft of the family, who fixed his refidence at
Ugbrooke, having inherited it in right of his
mother,

mother, the daughter and heirefs of Sir Pierce Courtenay of Chudleigh, brother of Sir William Courtenay of Powderham.

Ugbrooke, for local merit, ranks among the principal places in the county of Devon. The Father of the prefent Lord began and made great improvements, which he did not live to finifh, but yet fo far advanced, as to open a fpacious field for the defcriptive Mufe to fport in. On that ground the Poem of Ugbrooke Park was written and publifhed under his Lordfhip's patronage.

The Poem opens with a converfation, which occafionally paffed upon the fubject between his Lordfhip and the Author. After a fhort outline given of the country round, and mention made of feveral chief feats in the county, as worthy of a Poet's notice, the Author enters more minutely upon the internal beauties of Ugbrooke itfelf, and expatiates upon the various objects, that rife fucceffively in view, as he moves

round

round the Park. The circumftance of a Danifh
camp within the fence furnifhes him a fair op-
portunity of introducing, by way of Epifode,
the ravages once made in this country by that
barbarous people, and the overthrow they received from Alfred the Great. A comparative
view of that inward fatisfaction, which fprings
from the tranquil enjoyment of rural fcenes, and
a fketch of fome particular improvements made
in the Park and Manfion bring on the conclu-
fion of the Poem with a compliment to the different branches of the Clifford family.

TO THE READER.

Page 5, before the two laſt lines, ſhould be inſerted the following verſes :—

In vain ſhall *Lupton** boaſt, in vain partake
Of kindred ſcenes, that grace *Geneva's* lake,
Bid rocks give way, bid verdure clothe the ſteep,
And woods ſtand nodding o'er the foaming deep!

Page 11. The river *Teign* is written as it is always pronounced Teing.

Page 13. Inſtead of Stoford, read Stover.

* Seat of the Hon. Mr. Juſtice Buller.

UGBROOKE PARK.

AMIDST the charms *Devonia*'s fhore difplays
To tempt the Bard, and decorate his lays,
Why filent fits the *Mufe*, unftrung her lyre,
Her laurels wither'd, and extinct her fire?
On AVON's bank fhe once was taught to fing,
And as fhe fung, the vale was heard to ring.
There at her eafe fhe tried the rural ftrain,
And drew the dancing fhepherds to the plain.
Does verfe no more, does fong no longer warm,
Or have the fylvan Graces ceafed to charm?

The hill, the lawn, the woodland, and the glade,

The rock, and fonoriferous cafcade

Enchantingly invite. See mountains rife

Advancing with their woods to meet the fkies.

See winding vales in broken flopes defcend,

See, interfperfed with trees, the plains extend,

And join the diftant hills. Here hand in hand,

Diffufing gladnefs o'er a fertile land,

Pomona fmiles, with *Ceres* by her fide,

The fwain's refrefhing folace, and his pride.

Can fcenes like thefe, fo lavifhly difplay'd,

Be only meant for Contemplation's aid?

Thefe to the Mufe in vocal right belong;

The Mufe moft triumphs in defcriptive fong.

To thefe the royal Bard attuned his lays,

And *Sion*'s mount proclaim'd their Maker's praife.

Th' attractive grove immortal *Plato* fought;

There *Ariftotle* ranged his depth of thought.

So in the fhade befide fome murm'ring fpring,

Arms and the man young *Maro* learn'd to fing;

Pluck'd

Pluck'd from each fpray, from each infpiring bough
The facred wreath, ftill blooming on his brow.

Shall *Saltram*'s* plains no fprightly thought infufe,
Nor into fong awake the flumb'ring Mufe ?
Does *Fortefcue*'s gay hill † no more invite,
Tho' *Grenville*'s charms with *Clinton*'s tafte unite ?
Shall *Edgcumbe*'s mount,‡ with matchlefs glories hung,
Unnoticed ftand, neglefted and unfung ?
'Thy caftle, *Powderham*,§ no attention claim ?
Old *Powderham*'s glory, and a *Courtenay*'s name
May to the verfe thus patronifed impart
A grace, a charm above the reach of art.
Shall *Haldon*'s monument,‖ that lifts its head
In grateful mem'ry to the warlike dead,

* Seat of Lord Berringdon.
† Caftle-Hill, the feat of Earl Fortefcue, plann'd by Lord Clinton.
‡ Seat of Earl Mount Edgcumbe.
§ Seat of Lord Vifcount Courtenay.
‖ Erefted by Sir Robert Palk, Bart. to the memory of his friend General Lawrence.

O'er

O'er lands and feas its tow'ring height difplay,

Without the tribute of a fingle lay?

In charms unrivall'd fhall bright *Mamhead* ‖ fhine,

And yet not challenge one poetic line?

Each fmiling object gilds the cheerful fcene,

Seas, villas, rocks, and lawns for ever green

Woods nodding on the lofty mountain's brow,

And *Ifca* winding thro' the vale below.

Shall *Brixham*'s ftrand * glow in th' hiftoric page,

And brighter *Torr* no poet's pen engage?

Tho' hallow'd mitres glitter there no more,

The friendly *Abbey* † ftill adorns the fhore.

There verdant meads, there hills and wood confpire

To charm the fight and fan the Mufe's fire.

Wide-ftretching rocks majeftically bold

Th' embofom'd bay within the land infold.

‖ The feat of the Earl of Lifburne.
* The landing-place of King William.
† Torr-Abbey, the feat of George Cary, Efq.

There

There Britain's fleets fecure at anchor lie,

Hear tempefts howl, and all their rage defy.

There meek Religion's ancient Temple rofe,

How great, how fall'n, the mournful ruin fhows.

Of facrilege behold what heaps 'appear;

Nor blufh to drop the tributary tear.

Here ftood the font; here on high columns raifed

The dome extended ; there the altar blazed.

The fhatter'd aifles, with cluft'ring ivy hung,

The yawning arch, in rude confufion flung,

Sad-ftriking remnants of a former age,

To pity now might melt the fpoiler's rage.

Lo! funk to reft the wearied Vot'ry fleeps,

While o'er his urn the gloomy cyprefs weeps.

Here filent paufe, here draw the penfive figh,

Here mufing learn to live, here learn to die.

But why thus linger on the fea-beat fhore,

And abfent fcenes thro' diftant views explore ?

Why ·

Why fearch around for charms, when here alone

All charms in *Ugbrooke* are comprifed in one?

Oft has the Mufe, my Lord, as here fhe ftray'd,

With partial eyes thefe charming fcenes furvey'd.

Oft has fhe fondly wifh'd thefe fcenes to fing,

And in fhort effays tried her tender wing.

To wake her voice to harmony, each grace,

Each glowing feature of th' enchanting place

Perfuafively unite. Collected here

As in a point all nature's charms appear.

Hills ftrive with woods, with water woods agree,

Of *Devon*'s fcenes the grand epitome.

Oft rambling in her dreams, for dreams by night

Retrace the objects, that by day delight,

She feem'd to climb the high hill's length'ning way,

Skim thro' the vale, and round the foreft play.

Then roufe, fond Mufe: when *Ugbrooke* thus infpires,

No vulgar flame thy gen'rous bofom fires.

Dare

Dare to be bold : thy arduous end to gain,

As nature prompts, let judgment guide the ftrain.

Suit to the tafk thy lofty-founding voice,

And by thy numbers vindicate thy choice.

Where teeming Nature fpreads fuch richnefs round,

And paints with fuch variety the ground,

Where namelefs beauties crowd upon the fight,

And charms unequal equally delight,

The ftrains alike in unifon fhould flow,

Not ftiffly high or negligently low,.

But what thro' all invariably muft pleafe,

With unaffected dignity and eafe :

Should, like the place, bold Nature's art combine,

And art be nature ftill in ev'ry line.

Immortal thus fhall royal *Windfor* live,

Poffefs'd of all, that verfe and tafte can give.

Unfading honours fhall her foreft crown,

And pay the bard with what he gives, renown.

In local merit, lefs does *Ugbrooke* fhine,

Or claim lefs favour from the vocal Nine ?

Here

Here once great *Dryden* ftray'd: here crown'd with bays
To lift'ning nymphs he fung his Mantuan lays.

Bold as he fung, he felt new raptures roll
In ev'ry vein, and fwell his glowing foul.
Of woods and rocks the blended light and fhade,
The folemn grotto and romantic glade,
The chequer'd landfcape and furrounding fcenes
Of waving forefts, and immortal greens
Taught his bright mind with brighter fparks to glow,
And his bold verfe in bolder ftrains to flow.
At ev'ry ftep, where'er he turn'd his eyes,
Frefh charms he faw in quick fucceffion rife;
Hills mixt with hills, as if by magic found,
Start into form in fweet diforder round.
Save; where judicious Art held Nature's hand,
And fingle trees in fcatter'd beauty ftand,
Bold rifing woods ftill crowded on his view,
Clung to the rocks, and wonder'd how they grew.

Hence

Hence thro' the whole a noble air is thrown,

And *Ugbrooke* is for fylvan grandeur known.

Roufed at the thought, the Mufe with ardour ran,

Caught up her chorded lyre, and thus began.

When Nature firft traced out the vaft defign,

And with her greater works bade *Ugbrooke* fhine,

In ftile unufual was the plan fhe drew,

At once to pleafe and ftrike with fomething new.

Amid the Beautiful we here behold,

Each feature, as it rofe, is ftrong and bold.

Not indigefted or confufedly hurl'd,

But fair-proportion'd, as th' harmonious world,

The focial parts in one great view appear,

That form a whole both wild and regular.

To thofe, who judge by ftudied rules of art,

And make the whole fubfervient to a part,

Whofe tafte the neat parterre and formal line

Of flow'ring fhrubs and circling path confine,

No

No feemly grace th' unpolifh'd draught may fhow:
'Tis not for them the great Sublime to know.

Above the plain fee hills on hills arife,
New objects vary ftill, and ftill furprife.
O'er cultured vales our eyes unbounded roam
To wilds remote, and ftill confefs their home.
For no mark'd bounds the fev'ral parts control,
Hills, woods, and rocks, form one united Whole.
Steep *Haldon* here his fable ridge extends,
There *Dart*'s high *Torr* in cloud-capt pomp afcends.
Around th' horifon, broken and unev'n,
Dark mountains fpread, and hide the bending heav'n.
Quick as we move, they feemingly advance
To meet our fteps, and mingle in the dance;
Now fideways join, now back diffufedly flide
In rugged groups, and o'er the vale divide.
The lovely vale, diverfified with fields,
Amid the wafte a pleafing contraft yields.

There

There devious ſtreams their rapid tribute bring
T' enrich the current of majeſtic *Teing*.
The *Teing*, collected in his wat'ry force,
Between the mountains works his various courſe :
Now clad with greens conceals his ſilent flood,
Now ſkirts the mead, and dives within the wood :
Then murmurs on, and burſting into day,
O'er rocky fragments rolls his waves away :
But rolls not far, before he winds again,.
As loath to leave the faſcinating plain,.
When nobly flowing with a wider ſweep,
He joins the tide,. and ruſhes to the deep.

Sleek lowing herds along his borders feed,
Amidſt his flocks the ſhepherd tunes his reed.
Heart-cheering gladneſs breathes in ev'ry gale,
And induſtry with plenty ſtrows the vale.
No democratic cry, no lawleſs roar
Of raving Anarchy aſſails the ſhore.

No

No Gallic leveller's detefted plan,

No rude invader of the laws of man

Here whets the fteel, or lifts the murd'rous hand

Of life or wealth to rob the peaceful land.

But loyal fhouts from ev'ry hamlet round,

From ev'ry cot, and ev'ry tongue refound :

With hand and heart fupport the royal throne,

And in their *Sov'reign's* rights congratulate their own.

Teington and *Kerfwell* firft in order rife,

Their chalky turrets gleaming thro' the fkies.

Kings there, 'tis fung, once ftrove for martial fame ;

Each village ftill retains the kingly name.*

Next lofty *Hennock* crowns the mountain's height,

Here *Illfington* and *Bovey* greet our fight,

There *Denbury* † unfolds his camp, his wood,

His hills and rocks, diftain'd with Danifh blood.

* Kingfteington and Kingfkerfwell.
† Seat of Thomas Taylor, Efq.

Here

Here *Highweek*'s tow'r, the failor's landmark ftands,

There *Creftow*'s rock the bofky vale commands.

The heath e'en fhines, and with expenfive toil

Improving *Stoford** clothes th' ungrateful foil.

Here *Whiteway*† peeps, there pleafant *Ingsdon*‡ fmiles,

While *Brent*'s dim *Torr* our wand'ring eye beguiles.

Here fcreen'd from ftorms and blafts of wintry fkies,

In the deep fhade fequefter'd *Ideford* lies:

And here our fteps inviting *Chudleigh* leads

Thro' flow'ry fields and ever-blooming meads.

Here *Lewel*-woods with *Ugbrooke* hills unite,

How rich, how full, how prominent and bright!

Soft purling ftreams in wild meanders flow,

And fhelt'ring groves forbid the ftorm to blow.

In contraft with the fmiling *Villa*'s grace,

A rock there ftands, the guardian of the place.

* Seat of James Templar, Efq.
† Seat of Montagu Edmund Parker, Efq.
‡ Seat of Charles Hale, Efq.

With

With frowning front he seems to threat the sky,

As from his side the marble fragments fly.

His uncouth shape, by age and tempests torn,

Loose-pendent shrubs and shaggy weeds adorn.

On his high cliffs the browsing flocks appear.

To shrink within the clouds, and feed in air,

While pressing thro' the mazes of his wood,

Close at his feet descends the foaming flood.

Waked Echo hears the rushing waters bound,

And from her cave returns the rushing sound.

With bolder notes now raise the tuneful song,

To bolder scenes more tuneful notes belong.

Not nodding Pelion with his sylvan host,

Nor Ida's self a prouder sight can boast,

Than what yon Mount,* with forest honours crown'd,

Exhibits to his kindred mountains round.

* Mount-Pleasant, within the Park.

There

There thriving elms and aſh diſpute the prize
With ſturdier oaks, that brave the ſtormy ſkies.
Their ſpreading limbs with rich luxuriance bend,
Above the clouds their ſtately heads aſcend.
Sweet-ſcenting limes a ſofter hue diſplay,
And balmy firs perfume the dawn of day.
There, brought from Lebanon, the cedar ſhines,
Tranſalpine poplars, cheſnut, planes, and pines,
Broad-branching beech, and larch with ſpiry pride,
O'er a vaſt tribe of vulgar trees preſide.
Now bow'ring greens their woven ſhades unite,
That ſcarce admit the glimm'ring ſtreaks of light.
Now op'ning glades diſcloſe the puzzled way,
And cheer the proſpect with a blaze of day.
Thro' ſhapeleſs boughs we catch th' expanding view,
Thro' ev'ry change the varying ſcene purſue ;
Each growing charm with eager look explore,
And ſcan with freſh delight each feature o'er.

Not

Not so in ancient days appear'd the land,

When *Danish* rovers rush'd on *Teingmouth*'s strand.

Then on these hills were new encampments* seen,

And threat'ning lances gleam'd along the green.

The rampart here still undemolish'd stands,

The platform there the valley still commands,

The mould'ring outwork still its crescent shows,

Here sunk the ditch, and there the castle rose.

Where Danes once slaked their thirst, here weeps the rill

In gentle murmurs stealing down the hill.

Then were *Britannia*'s brighter days o'ercast,

Her towns a ruin, and her fields a waste.

Her plunder'd swains, untrain'd to war's alarms,

Nor taught the feats and exercise of arms,

To lonely deserts from their hamlets fled,

Or with their slaughter'd teems defenceless bled.

At length immortal *Alfred* raised his hand

To snatch from bondage freedom's native land.

* Danish camp in the park.

Aloft

Aloft in air the royal banner flew,

And round their Prince a hoft of heroes drew.

Arm'd for their country's good, along they prefs'd ;

With thirft of glory panted ev'ry breaft.

Swift as the bird of cloud-compelling Jove,

Upon the foe refiftlefs *Alfred* drove,

And bade the battle bleed.   Keen flafhes fly

From his broad fteel ; in heaps the vanquifh'd die.

On *Haldon* hill by his avenging fword,

Himfelf a hoft, fell *Denmark*'s fwarthy Lord.

Fierce as he fell, he rued the fatal wound,

Grinn'd in the pangs of death, and bit the ground.

From him the Down* derives its vulgar name,

The lafting monument of *Denmark*'s fhame.

To face the fight then *Danes* prefumed no more,

But fled the field, and fought the Baltic fhore.

Thus when the winds rufh'd from Æolia's plain

To wreck Æneas in the ftormy main,

---

* Hall-down commonly called Haldon.

Pale Trojans saw the gath'ring tempests sweep
Acrofs the sky, and settle on the deep.
The clouds now burst, now from the kindling pole
Red lightnings flash, and angry thunders roll.
Indignant *Neptune* heard the surges roar,
And in huge mountains break upon the shore:
Then calmly rising from the ruffled flood,
As round his car the sea-born *Tritons* stood,
With stern rebuke he bade the tumult ceafe,
Fly, winds, he cried; they fled, and all was peace.
So fell the war. *Britannia* smiled to see
Her King triumphant, and her people free:
Herself revered by all the nations round,
Alike for commerce as in arms renown'd.

But hark! what pealing shouts the forest cheer?
The fancied found still vibrates on the ear.
Lo! where the *Danes* had raifed the hostile mound,
Victorious *Britons*, now with laurel crown'd,

Their

Their joyous pæans in loud chorus fing;

The woods, the rocks, and hollow mountains ring.

Borne on the winds exulting pæans rife,

And float in fwelling triumph to the fkies.

With confcious warmth each hero's bofom glows,

And down his cheek the filent tranfport flows.

In tranfport loft each foldier had by chance

Around th' intrenchment fix'd his pointed lance:

The lance with mufic animated grew,

Off from its fpear the polifh'd metal flew.

Now ftrange to tell, quick ftrikes the fibrous root,

While high in air the fpreading branches fhoot.

The fmooth round trunk enclofing bark confines,

And in full bloom the burfting foliage fhines.

Thus, where a hoft of martial lances ftood,

In oval fhape now ftands the marfhall'd wood.

Hail, facred fhades, the Mufe's foft retreat,

The haunt of Wifdom, and the Graces feat,

Your

Your gueſt for life a friendly Bard receive ;.

'Tis all he aſks ; O grant,. if not, forgive.

Here let him ſing his unambitious lays,

Here ſteal thro' life, here cloſe his peaceful days.

So ſhall no ſlaught'ring ax, with ſtroke profane,.

Aſſault the honours of your ſylvan reign.

The trees, by luckleſs fate condemn'd to fall,.

From other hills let guilty gameſters call ;

Of yours not one the rueful die ſhall mourn,.

Nor from its ſtation be ignobly borne.

The great, the gay, now wild and thoughtleſs grown,

May whirl thro' all the follies of the town,

From plays to routs, from routs to maſquerades,

Turn night to day, and day to midnight ſhades.

But there life's pureſt joys they ne'er will know,.

Such as theſe flow'ry ſylvan ſcenes beſtow.

Unenvied let the Virtuoſi prize

Their birds, their inſects, grubs and butterflies ;

Bid

Bid lifelefs forms in dainty order lie,

And with ftuff'd mummies feed the taftelefs eye.

Here life itfelf more fprightly decks the day,

When on the lawn the hare and pheafant play,

Or when the deer, exulting with a bound,

Darts thro' the glade, and fprings along the ground.

O'er mouldy bufts let Antiquaries pore,

Of urns and coins the facred ruft adore;

Change fcores of *George's* for one *Otho's* face,

And learnedly enjoy the precious brafs.

Of ancient honours here, of long-lived fame

More modern marks our better homage claim.

Thefe rev'rend hills, with aged forefts crown'd,

Thefe groves, this fylvan majefty around,

Of fage progenitors to fons unborn

Shall mark the feat, and ftill the feat adorn.

This

This is the feat famed *Clifford** once admired,

'Twas here, too wife for ftate, he once retired.

Clifford, unawed by intereft or fear,

Hypocrify's falfe garb difdain'd to wear.

No flave to party or the fickle crowd,

The fchemes he plann'd, he publicly avow'd.

Friend to his King, by principle was juft,

Inflexible and fteady to his truft.

But when to private pique, and each vile end

The public weal was bafely made to bend,

When Honefty no more approach'd the throne,

Nor Loyalty her fentiments could own,

When to be great, men were no longer good,

And carelefs *Charles* went headlong with the flood,

Then the much-injured Treafurer withdrew,

Aftrea-like, nor courts nor courtiers knew.

* Lord HighTreafurer Clifford. See his character in Macpherfon.
Vol. 1.

Let fpeculative Sages range the fphere

Of heav'nly orbs, and trace the changing year

Fix motion's laws, explain attraction's force,

The caufe of thunder and the lightning's courfe ;

Say, round the lazy poles if oceans flow,

Or lands lie buried in eternal fnow ;

Tell, why the tides refpect their fandy bound,

And fear to trefpafs on forbidden ground.

'Tis yours, my Lord, to form the rural feat,

And add new luftre to your own retreat,

To model with the Genius of the place

Each leading feature, each fpontaneous grace,

To fhade the hill, to fcoop or fwell the green,

And break with wild diverfities the fcene.

For as you plan, the Genius ftill prefides,

Directs each ftroke, and each improvement guides.

Hence thro' the whole, irregularly great,

Nature and Art the wondrous work complete ;

In all fo true, fo unperceived the fkill,

That nature modified is nature ftill.

Obfequious ·

Obfequious rills unite their liquid ftore,

And fifhes fport, where vipers lurk'd before.

Diftinguifh'd from the reft a fountain flows,

That has no equal, and no rival knows.

A marble rock its copious ftream fupplies,

Thence fprings its fource, and there its treafure lies.

A concave form the fhelving fides betray,

And crowding trees exclude the folar ray.

Hence let *Arcturus* drench the hills with rain,

Or fiery *Cancer* parch with drought the plain,

'The limpid well an even current pours,

By funs not heated, nor diftain'd by fhow'rs.

Along the vale, adorn'd with lawn and wood,

Now winds the deep, the wide-extended flood.

Clear as the wave of *Torr*'s tranfparent bay,

When dazzling funbeams on its furface play,

The fmooth expanfe reflects a floating gleam

Of verdant flopes, that paint the lucid ftream.

Where

Where once they grazed, the wond'ring deer defcry
Inverted tow'rs, that meet the downward fky:
Then trembling ftart with wild furprife to hear
New founds of water rufhing on their ear.
Spent in the windings of the fkirting grove,
The ling'ring current fcarcely feems to move,
When lo! abruptly from the rocky fteep
Headlong it falls, and dafhes down the deep.
From crag to crag the tumbling waters bound,
And foam, and fret, and whirl their eddies round,
'Till by degrees in milder falls they play,
And in foft whifpers gently glide away.
Luxuriant oaks, by wanton nature bred,
Along the banks their waving honours fpread.

Now pleafed we turn, and fee the Manfion rife
With battlements and tow'rs, that emulate the fkies;
In ftile and plan fo fitted to the place,
That each on each reflects a fifter grace.

C   Let

Let loud *Pompofo* puff his villa's coft,

And brag the fums magnificently loft :

No pompous littlenefs thefe ftructures know,

Nor pile up vain extravagance for fhow.

Altho' no heaps of glittering expence

Our pride here flatter, or miflead our fenfe,

Altho' the wall no crowded paintings hide,

And no *Sir Jofhua* ftands by *Lely's* * fide ;

Altho' no colours on the canvafs glow,

But what a *Van Dyke*,† or a *Titian*‡ fhow,

A *Lint*,§ a *Rubens*,‖ or a *Guido's* ¶ ftile,

Or *Gentilefchi* **, in the *Virgin's* fmile ;

Altho' no figures load the ceiling's weight,

Nor gorgeous columns prop its falling height.

* A portrait of Lord Treafurer Clifford by Sir Peter Lely.
† A picture of the Tribute Money.
‡ The Adultrefs Woman and a Magdalen.
§ A picture of the Little Children by Peter Van Lint.
‖ A picture of the Virgin and Child.
¶ A Magdalen.
** A picture of the Holy Family.

Yet

Yet ftill there is, what more our judgment charms.

'Tis tafte, 'tis manly elegance, that warms

And dignifies the whole.   Thus rofe the plan,

Thus *Adams* modell'd what you firft began.

No more let *Phrygia* boaft her needle's grace,

Nor beds of ftate in *Tyrian* colours trace ;

But here her fkill and all her art forego,

Here gaze with envy or with rapture glow.

See,* on the filken ground how *Flora* pours

Her various dies and opulence of flow'rs ;

How, blended with the foliage of the rofe

And rich carnation, the ftreak'd tulip blows.

The downy peach and curling vine appear

With all the treafures of the purple year.

Poifed on her velvet plumes of vivid green,

The Paroquet enlivens here the fcene ;

With half-expanded wing there fits the Dove

In rifing attitude ; intent above

* The ftate bed.

She

She turns her eye, where on extended wings
Thro' fields of air her lively confort fprings.
With yellow crefts the Cockatoos unfold
Their milky plumage, ftain'd with tints of gold.
Here frefh as life in all their glory dreft,
The bold Maccaws difplay the fcarlet breaft,
The painted neck of variegated hue,
And glofly wings of bright cerulean blue.

This graceful *Norfolk*'s * fkill alone could teach,
This fuch is fate, no other hand fhall reach.
This, the rich emblem of her noble mind,
For *Norfolk*'s heir fhe traced, at once defign'd
A monument of tafte. Alafs, how vain
Are oft our fchemes. how mixt with feeds of pain
Are half our joys ! In life no fooner known,
But, as a lily cut untimely down,
Howard † was fnatch'd away. With him expired
My hope, fhe faid, and all I once defired.

* Maria, Dutchefs of Norfolk.
† Edward Howard, Efq. fon of the Hon. Philip Howard by
his fecond wife, the fifter of her Grace of Norfolk.

In him kind Heav'n had ev'ry gift combin'd,
That forms the heart, and trains the virtuous mind.
Howard—a name ftill fad, yet ever dear—
And at the name out gufh'd the big round tear :
O *Clifford,* now my fecond hope, receive
This laft beft pledge *Maria's* hand can give.
So fhall I fmile, howe'er by fortune croft,
In you to find the work has not been loft.

She faid : and *Ugbrooke* to his fplendid ftore
Added this one unequall'd treafure more.
Th' affenting Genius fmiled, was glad to fee
Art ftill with nature vie, and ftill agree.
Alike in all thus Art and Nature grace
With neat, with rich fimplicity the place.

No ftiff formality, no noife or ftrife
Here cloud the day, or damp the joys of life.
Each cheerful morn, with eafe and plenty ftored,
Spreads for each welcome gueft the friendly board.

C 2   No

No plaintive figh heaves from the forrow'd breaft,

But Pity feels and comforts the diftrefs'd :

Supports pale Sicknefs on her bed of grief,

Prepares the med'cine and imparts relief :

To helplefs Age and Want divides the bread,

And bids Defpondence raife her drooping head.

Thanks to the hand, from whence fuch bounties flow,

With heart-felt joy the grateful Poor beftow.

Hence on the noble *Pair* in fhow'rs defcend

The pureft bleffings Heav'n itfelf can fend.

Domeftic virtues in fair order move,

Connubial faith, and harmony and love.

Hence of celeftial Pow'rs the fav'rite care,

May all their offspring all thofe bleffings fhare !

May to their own their Parents virtues join,

And with new luftre fwell the *Clifford* line !

Blithe as the morn, and as *Narciffus* fair,

In bloom of youth behold the rifing *Heir !*

In

In converſe gay, in ſentiment refined,

In manners courteous, friend to all mankind.

That ſprightly life, which ſparkles in his eye,

That captivating air—ſoon, ſoon muſt die.

Beſide his couch in vain his *Conſort* kneels,

Con oles his pains, and ev'ry ſorrow feels.

With many an anxious thought, and many a ſigh,

Thro' all the changes of a foreign ſky,

By love, by friendſhip, and by duty led,

For him ſhe had from ev'ry comfort fled,

For him had ſought, what titles, honours, wealth

Could ne'er command, the firſt of bleſſings, health:

'Till worn and ſpent, and lab'ring now for breath,

She ſees him fainting in the arms of death.

No help, no friend, no confident is near

To ſooth her grief or catch the falling tear.

As a tall poppy, when o'ercharged with rain,

Bends drooping down, and ſinks upon the plain,

So ſunk the *Peer*—in life to ſhine no more,

Conſign'd to duſt on *Munich*'s diſtant ſhore.

There

There while he fleeps, let hallow'd tapers burn,
And Angels watch around his fculptured urn.

From the ftill fhade of fweet domeftic life,
Unknown to envy and ambitious ftrife,
Now firft in rank fteps forth the fecond *Son*
To finifh what his active *Sire* begun.
With him a *Nymph** of *Wardour's* princely dome
To fix the Graces in their ancient home
His pleafing *Confort* comes : their joy, their care
A blooming *Offspring* crowns the happy *Pair.*
Away our forrows at the profpect fly,
And bright'ning tranfports beam in ev'ry eye.
Reviving *Ugbrooke* cafts his broken plumes,
His former ftate and dignity refumes.

* The daughter of Lord Arundell of Wardour.

C A T O.

A TRAGEDY.

By Mr. ADDISON.

———◆———

DONE INTO LATIN VERSE

WITHOUT THE LOVE SCENES.

C 5   CATO.

C A T O.

A

TRAGEDY.

By Mr. ADDISON.

WITHOUT THE

LOVE SCENES.

———

SECOND EDITION.

———

*Ecce fpeɛtaculum dignum, ad quod refpiciat, intentus operi fuo,
Deus! Ecce par Deo dignum, vir fortis cum malâ fortunâ
compofitus! Non video, inquam, quid habeat in terris Jupiter
pulchrius, fi convertere animum velit, quàm ut fpeɛtet Catonem,
jàm partibus non femel fraɛtis, nihilominùs inter ruinas pub-
licas ereɛtum.*

SEN. de Divin. Prov.

C A T O.

TRAGOEDIA.

AUTORE CLARISSIMO VIRO

JOSEPHO ADDISON,

Inter Angliæ noſtræ principes Poëtas

JURE NUMERANDO

OMISSIS AMATORIIS SCENIS,

LATINO CARMINE VERSA.

EDITIO SECUNDA.

Ecce ſpeEtaculum dignum, ad quod reſpiciat, intentus operi ſuo Deus ! Ecce par Deo dignum, vir fortis cum malâ fortunâ cumpoſitus! Non video, inquam, quid habeat in terris Jupiter pulchrius, ſi convertere animum velit, quàm ut ſpeEtet Catonem, jam partibus non ſemel fraEtis, nihilominùs inter ruinas pub-licas ereEtum.

SEN. d. Divin. Prov.

To the READER.

Voltaire sur la Tragedie Angloise.

M. Voltaire in his remarks on the English Tragedy, thus speaks of Mr. Addison's Cato.

Le Caton de Mr. Addison me paroit le plus beau personnage, qui soit sur aucun Théatre; mais les autres rôles de la piece n'y repondent pas; & cet ouvrage si bien écrit est défiguré par un intrigue froide d'amour, qui repand sur la piece une langueur, qui la tuë.

La coûtume d'introduire de l'amour à tort & à travers dans les ouvrages dramatiques, passa de Paris a Londres vers l'an 1660 avec nos rubans & nos perruques. Les femmes qui parent les spectacles, comme ici, ne veulent plus souffrir qu'on leur parle d'autre chose que d'amour. Le sage Addison eût la molle complaisance de plier la severité de son caractére aux mœurs de son tems, & gâta un chef d'œuvre pour avoir voulu plaire.

Mr.

MR. ADDISON's CATO is, in my opinion, the greateft character, that ever appeared on the ftage; but the inferior parts of the play are no ways anfwerable to it. That excellent work is disfigured by an infipid intrigue, which, by the extreme fiatnefs of it, murders the whole piece.

The cuftom of introducing love, right or wrong, upon the ftage, paffed from Paris to London about the year 1660, with our ribands and perukes. The ladies, who grace the public appearance at theatrical exhibitions there, as they do here, will hear nothing but love. The grave ADDISON was fo weak, as to fubmit his auftere genius to the manners of the age, and, out of a defire to pleafe, fpoiled a mafterly performance.

THE intent of the Tranflator being to fet forth the generous fentiments of the Roman Patriot in a language he formerly fpoke, greater care has been taken to preferve the dignity of thought and expreffion, than to give a verbal tranflation.

Nec

Nec verbo verbum curabit reddere fidus
Interpres . . . . Hor.

The Love Scenes being entirely out, it has been neceffary here and there to make fome fmall change in the original expreffion, and fometimes to borrow verfes from different fcenes, to make the tranfition and connection of the parts natural.

In the margin are marked the chief changes and the places, where the verfes are to be found, which in this verfion are read in other fcenes.

DRAMATIS

DRAMATIS PERSONÆ.

CATO,

LUCIUS, ... SENATOR.

SEMPRONIUS, ... SENATOR.

JUBA, ... NUMIDIÆ *Princeps.*

SYPHAX, ... *Dux* NUMIDARUM.

PORCIUS, ...
MARCUS, ... } CATONIS *Filii.*

DECIUS, ... *Legatus à* CÆSARE.

Nuncius, Seditiofi, Satellites, &c.

SCENA UTICÆ *in Prætorio.*

CATO.

C A T O.

ACT I. — SCENE I.

PORCIUS, MARCUS.

PORCIUS.

THE dawn is over-caſt, the morning low'rs,
And heavily in clouds brings on the day,
The great, th' important day, big with the fate
Of *Cato*, and of Rome.   Our father's death
Would fill up all the guilt of civil war,
And cloſe the ſcene of blood.   Already Cæſar
Has ravag'd more than half the globe, and ſees
Mankind grown thin by his deſtructive ſword.

Should

C A T O.

═

ACTUS PRIMUS. — SCENA PRIMA.

PORCIUS, MARCUS.

PORCIUS.

OBTECTA dubium nube fqualenti jubar
Aurora terris revehit exoriens diem
Inaufpicatum, lugubri fato gravem
Romæ & Catonis.   Patris effufus cruor
Civilis omne penitus impleret nefas,
Clademque belli.   Parte plus mediâ infolens
Orbis fubactâ, Cæfar humanum genus
Rarefcere videt marte deletum impio.

Should he go further, numbers would be wanting

To form new battles, and support his crimes.

Ye gods, what havock does ambition make

Among your works!

MARCUS.

Thy steady temper, Porcius,

Can look on guilt, rebellion, fraud, and Cæsar,

In the calm lights of mild philosophy.

I'm tortured, even to madness, when I think

On the proud victor. Ev'ry time he's nam'd,

Pharsalia rises to my view. I see

Th' insulting tyrant prancing o'er the field

Strow'd withRome's citizens, and drench'd in slaughte

His horse's hoofs wet with Patrician blood.

Oh Porcius, is there not some chosen curse,

Some hidden thunder in the stores of heav'n,

                                        Red

Si porrò pergat, terra, jam propè incolis
Exhausta, tantis criminum haud ultrà queat
Sufficere monstris.　Quanta, proh superi, mala
Invexit orbi dira regnandi sitis !

MARCUS.

Virtute nixus Stoicâ has rerum vices,
Hæc sæva patriæ busta tranquillo potes
Animo intueri.　Mente ego insanâ feror,
Quoties superbi imago victoris subit.
Quoties ad aures Cæsaris nomen venit,
Thessalica toties arva Romano ebria
Cruore, toties cæde bacchantem ferâ
Cernere tyrannum videor.　Insultans equo
Vehitur per aciem civibus stratam suis,
Humilíque mixtos plebe patricios duces
Cruentus obterit ungulâ.　O, si quod polo est
Fulmen repostum, fulmen insueto rubens
Furore, Porci, nubibus ruptis micet,
Viríque flammâ vindice involvat caput,

Qui

Red with uncommon wrath, to blaſt the man,

Who owes his greatneſs to his country's ruin ?

PORCIUS.

Believe me, Marcus, 'tis an impious greatneſs,

And mix'd with too much horror to be envied.

How does the luſtre of our father's actions,

Through the dark cloud of ills, that cover him,

Break out, and burn with more triumphant brightneſs ?

His ſuff'rings ſhine, and ſpread a glory round him.

Greatly unfortunate, he fights the cauſe

Of honour, virtue, liberty, and Rome.

MARCUS.

Who knows not this ? But what can Cato do

Againſt a world, a baſe degen'rate world,

That courts the yoke, and bows the neck to Cæſar ?

Pent up in Utica, he vainly forms

A

Qui per ruinas patriæ ſternit ſibi

Iter ad honores!

PORCIUS.

Ille, mihi crede, impio

Qui ſcelere paritur, ſplendidè mendax honor

Haud invidendus fuerit. O quantò magis

Operoſa patris inclyti virtus nitet!

Spiſsâ malorum nube depreſſus licèt

Multa aſpera tulit, major è dubiis tamen

Micuit procellis, luce conſpicuus novâ.

Multa quoque bello paſſus, infelix ſacra

Dum jura libertatis & Romæ aſſerit.

MARCUS.

Nemo iſta neſcit. Quid tamen *Cato* poteſt

Solus, ubi Roma degener & iners ſibi

Servile patitur facilis imponi jugum?

Incluſus Uticæ mœnibus fruſtrà ſtudet

Fulcire lapſum Romuli imperii decus.

Milite Numidio cinctus exiguam regit

Umbram

A poor epitome of Roman greatnefs,

And, cover'd with Numidian guards, directs

A feeble army and an empty fenate,

Remnants of mighty battles fought in vain.

By heav'ns, fuch virtues, join'd with fuch fuccefs,

Diftract my very foul. Our father's fortune

Would almoft tempt us to renounce his precepts.

PORCIUS.

Remember, what our father oft has told us.

The ways of heav'n are dark and intricate,

Puzzled in mazes, and perplex'd with errors.

Our underftanding traces 'em in vain,

Loft and bewilder'd in the fruitlefs fearch ;

Nor fees with how much art the windings run,

Nor where the regular confufion ends.

MARCUS.

Thefe are fuggeftions of a mind at eafe.

Oh Porcius, did'ft thou tafte but half the griefs,

That

Umbram fenatûs, fractaque virorum agmina,

Tenues reliquias Cæfaris, in aciem trahit.

Dii, tanta virtus dum malis tantis jacet

Oppreffa, lancinat intimum pectus delor.

Hæc fi Catonis pretia virtutem manent,

Quis non Catonis penè dubitaret fequi

Præcepta, Porci?

PORCIUS.

Sæpè nos docuit pater

Confilia fuperûm mille mæandros, finus

Habere mille, mille & errorum vias.

Unde inchoetur, vel ubi fefe ordo explicet

Indeprehenfus, laffa mens nequit affequi.

Caliginofâ nocte fed preffum latet,

Quicquid removit ab acie humanâ Deus.

MARCUS.

Tranquillioris fenfa mentis ifta funt.

Me mille curæ, multiplex me angit dolor.

O chare Porci, tale fi quidquam modò

Paterêre,

That wring my foul, thou could'ft not talk thus coldly.

Such an unlook'd-for ftorm of ills falls upon me,*

It beats down all my ftrength.   I cannot bear it.

PORCIUS.

Now, Marcus, now thy virtue's on the proof.

Put forth thy utmoft ftrength, work ev'ry nerve,

And call up all thy father in thy foul.

To quell thy fears and guard thy drooping heart

On this weak fide, where moft our nature fails,

Would be a conqueft worthy *Cato's* fon.

MARCUS.

Porcius, the counfel, which I cannot take,

Inftead of healing, but upbraids my weaknefs.

Bid me for honour plunge into a war

Of thickeft foes, and rufh on certain death,

Then fhalt thou fee, that Marcus is not flow

To follow glory, and confefs his father.

---

* Thefe two verfes are taken out of the fecond fcene of the third act, where Porcius fpeaks.

But

Paterêre, non fic mente compofitâ anxia
Tempora loquendo falleres. Impar malis
Animus ferendis deficit, labat, cadit.

PORCIUS.

Dii fic virile pectus ærumnis probant.
Macte ergo virtute novâ, age omnes impiger
Intende nervos, & animi vim omnem advoca,
Totúmque patrem. Vincere imbelles metus,
Sortémque forti pectore adverfam pati,
Magni Catonis filium & juvat & decet.

MARCUS.

Confilia capere indocilis ægrefcit magis
Animus medendo. Ruere in hoftiles globos
Laurúmque petere morte venalem jube;
Haud unquam ab altâ laude degenerem patris
Marcum videbis. Inultus aft ubi mala

D   . Circùm

But when I fee fuccefs ftill follows Cæfar,

And ftill backs his crimes, when I fee fuch virtue

Afflicted by the weight of fuch misfortunes,

Life hangs upon me and becomes a burden. *

PORCIUS.

Behold young Juba, the Numidian prince !

With how much care he forms himfelf to glory,

And breaks the fiercenefs of his native temper

To copy out our father's bright example.

What, fhall an African, fhall Juba's heir

Reproach great *Cato*'s fon, and fhew the world

A virtue wanting in a Roman foul ?

MARCUS.

Porcius, no more. Your words leave ftings behind 'em.

Whene'er did Juba, or did Porcius, fhew

A virtue, that has caft me at a diftance,

And thrown me out in the purfuits of honour ?

---

* Vide the firft and fourth fcene of act II. where Cato fpeaks ;
and the firft fcene of act III. where Marcus fpeaks.

PORCIUS.

Circùm ingruentia cerno, ubi fata & deos

Cerno ufque placidos Cæfari, iratos piis,

Mœrore feffum lucis æthereæ piget.

PORCIUS.

Sufpice Numidiæ principem : en quanto flagrans

Amore gloriæ indolem feram domat,

Noftri parentis æmulus.   Fato altior

Inter cadentes fortis adverfæ minas

Veftigia patris paffibus anhelis legit.

Quid, an Catonis filius cedet Jubæ ?

Romanus Afro ?

MARCUS.

Parce plura : acres finu

Stimulos fub alto figis.   Ecquando Juba,

Ecquando Porcius ipfe me pigrum arguit

Honoris ?

PORCIUS.

Marcus, I know thy gen'rous temper well.

Fling but th' appearance of diſhonour on it,

It ſtraight takes fire, and mounts into a blaze.

MARCUS.

A brother's ſuff'rings claim a brother's pity.

PORCIUS.

Heav'n knows, I pity thee.   Behold my eyes ;

Ev'n whilſt I ſpeak . . . . do they not ſwim in tears ?

Were but my heart as naked to thy view,

Marcus would ſee it bleed in his behalf.

MARCUS.

Why then doſt treat me with rebukes, inſtead

Of kind condoling cares, and friendly ſorrow ?

PORCIUS.

O Marcus, did I know the way to eaſe

Thy troubled heart, and mitigate thy pains,

Marcus, believe me, I could die to do it.

MARCUS.

PORCIUS.

Eſt generoſa mihi nota indoles.

Vel ipſa tenuis umbra te totum excitat,

Dedecoris ipſum nomen in flammas rapit.

MARCUS.

A fratre lachrymas poſtulat fratris dolor.

PORCIUS.

Conteſtor aſtra, Marce, me miſeret tui.

Hæc cerne lumina: nonne dum loquor, madent

Perfuſa fletu? O ſi tibi nudum quoque

Cor hoc pateret, cerneres totum tuo

Dolore ſaucium.

MARCUS.

Ergo quid plagam aſperas,

Et non amicâ mitigas potiùs manu?

PORCIUS.

Ter chare frater, fare, ſi quæ te premunt,

Hâc te levare mole curarum queam.

Equidem vel ipſâ morte fraternos velim

Redimere luctus.

MARCUS.

MARCUS.

Thou best of brothers, and thou best of friends !
Pardon a weak diftemper'd foul, that fwells
With fudden gufts, and finks as foon in calms,
The fport of paffions. But Sempronius comes.
He muft not find this foftnefs hanging on me.

[Exit.

SCENE

O mihi frater fide

Junôte Pyladeâ, parce turbato malis

Animo, ac dolori facilis indulge meo.

Sempronius venit : animi hunc mollem decet

Celare luôtum.

[Exit.

SCENA.

SCENE II.

ENTER SEMPRONIUS.

SEMPRONIUS.

CONSPIRACIES no fooner fhould be form'd,
Than executed.   What means Porcius here?
I like not that cold youth.   I muft diffemble,
And fpeak a language foreign to my heart.

[*Afide.*

SEMPRONIUS, PORCIUS.

Good morrow Porcius!   Let us once embrace,
Once more embrace, whilft yet we both are free:
To-morrow fhould we thus exprefs our friendfhip,
Each might receive a flave into his arms.
This fun' perhaps, this morning fun's the laft,
That e'er fhall rife on Roman liberty.

PORCIUS.

SCENA SECUNDA.

SEMPRONIUS.

UBI agitur aut vita aut falus,
Confilia nullum capta patiuntur moram.
Verùm quid ifthic Porcius ? Oportet, vafer
Arcana cordis fronte fimulatâ tegam.

[*Seorfim.*

SEMPRONIUS, PORCIUS.

Salveto, Porci ! Mutuo amplexu frui
Dum liberis licet, in tuum finum ruo.
Si cras eandem fortè teftemur fidem,
Uterque fervum in brachia accipiat fua.
Hodierna forfan ultima hæc venit dies,
Quæ Romuli urbem cernat immunem jugo.

PORCIUS.

PORCIUS.

My father has this morning call'd together

To this poor hall his little Roman senate,

The leavings of Pharsalia, to consult

If yet he can oppose the mighty torrent,

That bears down Rome, and all her gods before it,

Or must at length give up the world to Cæsar.

SEMPRONIUS.

Not all the pomp and majesty of Rome

Can raise her senate more than *Cato*'s presence.

His virtues render our assembly awful.

They strike with something like religious fear,

And make ev'n Cæsar tremble at the head

Of armies flush'd with conquest. O my Porcius !

The world has all its eyes on *Cato*'s son.

Thy father's merit sets thee up to view,

And shews thee in the fairest point of light,

To make thy virtues, or thy faults, conspicuous.

PORCIUS.

PORCIUS.

Parvum fenatum juffit hodierno pater

Mane huc coire, & quid ftatu hoc rerum juvet,

Confulere fecum : an quâ arte pervinci queat

Fortuna, fitne aliquando cedendum malis,

Queis funt refiftendo impares Roma atque Dii.

SEMPRONIUS.

Confilia præfens noftra cùm *Cato* regit,

Secura pofito Roma refpirat metu :

Victórque vel dum bella per mundum vehit,

Tremit ipfe Cæfar.   Quin age & tu aude quoque

Virtute, Porci, in fimile conniti decus.

Magni Catonis fama præclufit tibi

Latebras inertes.   Judices in te omnium

Vertuntur oculi, nobili an dignum patre,

Laudifne degenerem, in tuâ fitum eft manu.

PORCIUS.

PORCIUS.

Well doft thou feem to check my ling'ring here
On this important hour ..... I'll ftraight away,
And while the fathers of the fenate meet
In clofe debate to weigh th' events of war,
I'll animate the foldiers' drooping courage,
With love of freedom, and contempt of life.
I'll thunder in their ears their country's caufe,
And try to roufe up all that's Roman in 'em.
'Tis not in mortals to command fuccefs,
But we'll do more, Sempronius ; we'll deferve it.

[*Exit.*

SEMPRONIUS Solus.

Curfe on the ftripling ! How he apes his fire ?
Ambitioufly fententious ! ...... But I wonder
Old Syphax comes not. His Numidian genius
Is well difpofed to mifchief, were he prompt
And eager on it ; but he muft be fpurr'd,
And ev'ry moment quicken'd to the courfe:
Cato has ufed me ill. He has refufed

His

PORCIUS.

Benè monuisti : me pigræ quanquam moræ

Ipsa nimis arguit hora. Militum ociùs

Turmas adibo, dumque conveniunt patres,

Monendo quidquid potero, ad arma desides

Animos ciebo : gloriæ accensos siti

Hortabor acres tendere in bella & neces

Patriæ atque libertatis ultores suæ.

Certos, amice, nemo successus potest

Sibi arrogare ; at nos, quod est honestius,

Merebimur virtute.

[*Exit.*

SEMPRONIUS Solus.]

Malè pereat puer

Sententiosus ! Ut animum affectat patris

Tumidúmque fastum ! Sed ubi cunctatur Syphax ?

Vafer ille Numida scelere fœcundum gerit

Aptúmque pectus, ni usque ad inceptum foret

Stimulo incitandus. Me malè accepit *Cato.*

Meritis

His daughter Marcia to my ardent vows.

Befides, his baffled arms and ruin'd caufe

Are bars to my ambition.   Cæfar's favour,

That fhow'rs down greatnefs on his friends, will raife me

To Rome's firft honours.

[*Syphax enters.*

SCENE

Meritis minorem retulit ingratus vicem.

Superbientis tanta faſtidia viri

Non ſunt ferenda. Me ſibi generum negat.

Dum Marte porrò fractus adverſo jacet,

Ambitio nullam eluſa mercedem feret.

Sin Cæſaris caſtra ſequor, ad primos patet

Aditus honores.

[*Ingreditur Syphax.*

SCENA

SCENE III.

SYPHAX, SEMPRONIUS.

SYPHAX.

SEMPRONIUS, all is ready.
I've founded my Numidians, man by man,
And find them ripe for a revolt. They all
Complain aloud of *Cato*'s difcipline,
And wait but the command to change their mafter.

SEMPRONIUS.

Believe me, Syphax, there's no time to wafte.
Even whilft we fpeak our conqueror comes on,
And gathers ground upon us ev'ry moment.
Alas! thou know'ft not Cæfar's active foul.
With what a dreadful courfe he rufhes on
From war to war! In vain has nature form'd
Mountains and oceans to oppofe his paffage.
He bounds o'er all, victorious in his march.

The

SCENA TERTIA.

SYPHAX, SEMPRONIUS.

SYPHAX.

CUNCTA pro votis eunt,

Numidas viritim voce compellans meos,

Quæ cuique mens fit, quæve, tentavi, fides.

Duce fub *Catone* gravia militiæ palam

Munia queruntur, & alium extemplò fequi

Uno propè omnes ore depofcunt ducem.

SEMPRONIUS.

Mihi crede, nullam tempus admittit moram.

Amice, vel dum loquimur, armorum ingruens

In nos procellâ propiùs huc victor tonat.

Proh quantus ardor impetu vafto omnia

Latè ruentem Cæfarem in bellum rapit !—

Natura fruftrà montium objecit moras,

Fruftrà æftuantia pandit oceanus vada.

Per

The Alps and Pyreneans fink before him.

Thro' winds and waves, and ftorms he works his way,

Impatient for the battle.   One day more

Will fet the victor thund'ring at our gates..

But tell me, haft thou yet drawn o'er young Juba?

That ftill would recommend thee more to Cæfar,

And challenge better terms.

SYPHAX.

Alas ! he's loft.

He's loft, Sempronius.   All his thoughts are full

Of *Cato*'s virtues.   But I'll try once more,

For ev'ry inftant I expect him here,

If yet I can fubdue thofe ftubborn principles

Of faith, of honour, and I know not what,

That have corrupted his Numidian temper,

And ftruck th' infection into all his foul.

SEMPRONIUS.

Be fure to prefs upon him ev'ry motive.

Juba's furrender, fince his father's death,

Would

Per mare, per ignes, pérque ventorum minas
Molitus iter in prœlia impatiens ruit.
Alpéfque Pyrenæque fubmittunt juga,
Facilémque fternunt faxa properanti viam.
His fortè muris victor infultet prius,
Quàm fol fub undas craftinum condat diem.
Sed age, approbatne noftra confilia Juba?

SYPHAX.

Heu fpes inanes! Pertinax juveni furor,
Æquum, fidefque, & nefcio quid animum abftulit.
Adeò in Catonem cæcus & præceps amor
Penitùs per omnes toxicum infudit fibras,
Rectumque Numidam tetricâ infecit lue.
Brevî affuturum expecto: rigidum denuò
Tentabo pectus.

SEMPRONIUS.

Omnia exploret Syphax.
Noftri attrahatur confilî in partem Juba,
Victoriífque adjecta veteribus Africa

Zonæ

Would give up Afric into Cæfar's hands,
And make him lord of half the burning zone.

SYPHAX.

But is it true, Sempronius, that your fenate
Is call'd together ? Gods ! thou muft be cautious !
· *Cato* has piercing eyes, and will difcern
Our frauds, unlefs they're cover'd thick with art.

SEMPRONIUS.

Let me alone, good Syphax.   I'll conceal
My thoughts in paffion ; 'tis the fureft way.
I'll bellow out for Rome, and for my country,
And mouth at Cæfar, 'till I fhake the fenate.
Your cold hypocrify's a ftale device,
A worn-out trick. Would'ft thou be thought in earneft
Clothe thy feign'd zeal in rage, in fire, in fury.

SYPHAX.

In troth, thou'rt able to inftruct grey hairs,
And teach the wily African, deceit !

SEMPRONIUS.

Zonæ rubentis Cæfarem latè dabit

Dominum potentem.

SYPHAX.

Sed hodiè nunquid *Cato*

Cogit fenatum ? Di ! effe te cautum decet.

Oculo fagaci cuncta periuftrans *Cato*

Confilia noftra perfpiciet, altâ nifi

Tegantur arte.

SEMPRONIUS.

Ne metue Syphax : mihi

Sat ifta curæ. Mente fimulatâ vafer

Amore patriæ fenfa velabo mea,

In Cæfarémque mille jactabo probra,

Donec labantes fando permoveam patres.

Se nempe feriò agere quis credi velit ?

Furore cæcos igneo fenfus tegat,

Certámque fictis afferet verbis fidem.

SYPHAX.

Solertiam herclè mente verfutâ potes

Vincere fenilem, & fraude fallacem novâ

Afrum erudire.

SEMPRONIUS.

SEMPRONIUS.

Once more be fure, to try thy fkill on Juba,
Mean while I'll haften to my Roman foldiers,
Inflame the mutiny, and underhand
Blow-up their difcontents, 'till they break out
Unlook'd for, and difcharge themfelves on *Cato.*
Remember, Syphax, we muft work in hafte.
O think, what anxious moments pafs between
The birth of plots, and their laft fatal periods.
Oh! 'tis a dreadful interval of time,
Fill'd up with horror all, and big with death!
Deftruction hangs on ev'ry word we fpeak,
On ev'ry thought, 'till the concluding ftroke
Determines all, and clofes our defign.

[*Exit.*

SYPHAX Solus.

I'll try if yet I can reduce to reafon
This headftrong youth, and make him fpurn at *Cato.*
The time is fhort, Cæfar comes rufhing on us....
But hold! young Juba fees me, and approaches.

SCENE

SEMPRONIUS.

Sed tu inexpertum nihil,

Tu nihil inaufum linque, & indictum nihil.

Ego ad maniplos interim pergam meos,

Animófque vulgi facibus accendam novis,

Donec inopino turbine Catonem obruant.

Qui fis, Syphax, memento : properato eft opus.

O quanta, nofti, cura follicitum tenet,

Dum pendet anceps facinus.   Auctori fuo

Incepta, non perafta confilia nocent.

[*Exit.*

SYPHAX Solus.

Urgenda res eft.   Cæfar & bellum ingruit.

Malè obftinatum flectere in melius Jubam

Tentabo rurfus, ínque Romanum afperis

Incendere odiis.

SCENA

SCENE IV.

JUBA, SYPHAX.

JUBA.

SYPHAX, I joy to meet thee thus alone.
I have obferved of late thy looks are fall'n,
O'ercaft with gloomy cares and difcontent.
Then tell me, Syphax, I conjure thee tell me,
What are the thoughts, that knit thy brow in frowns,
And turn thine eye thus coldly on thy prince?

SYPHAX.

'Tis not my talent to conceal my thoughts,
Or carry fmiles and fun-fhine in my face,
When difcontent fits heavy at my heart.
I have not yet fo much the Roman in me.

JUBA.

Why doft thou caft out fuch ungen'rous terms
Againft the lords and fov'reigns of the world?

Do'lt

SCENA QUARTA.

JUBA, SYPHAX.

JUBA.

COMMODE' occurris, Syphax,
Mihi expetitus. Ecqua rugofam afperat
Ægra tibi frontem cura? Cur folito magis
Mœftùm íntueris capite demiſſo folum?

SYPHAX.

Fallace rifus ore ſimulatos dare,
Cùm triſtis intus infidet menti dolor,
Nec ingenî, nec artis eſt opus meæ.
Romanus adeò eſſe nequeo.

JUBA.

Ita rerum arbitros
Dominófque quorfum dente mordaci petis?

E   Romana

Doſt thou not ſee mankind fall down before them,

And own the force of their ſuperior virtue?

Is there a nation in the wilds of Afric,

Amidſt our barren rocks, and burning ſands,

That does not tremble at the Roman name?

SYPHAX.

Gods! where's the worth that ſets this people up

Above your own Numidia's tawny ſons?

Do they with tougher ſinews bend the bow,

Or flies the jav'lin ſwifter to its mark,

Launch'd from the vigour of a Roman arm?

Who like our active African inſtructs

The fiery ſteed, and trains him to his hand?

Or guides in troops th' embattled elephant,

Loaden with war? Theſe, theſe are arts, my prince,

In which your Zama does not ſtoop to Rome.

JUBA.

Theſe all are virtues of a meaner rank;

Perfections, that are plac'd in bones and nerves.

A

Romana nunquid arma, virtutes, viros

Victus stupescit orbis & adorat decus?

Quæ gens arenas Africæ & syrtes colit,

Quæ non vel ipsum nomen Ausonium tremit?

SYPHAX.

Virtute Numidis, quæso, quâ tandem tuis

Gens illa præstat? Promptior an hostem ferit?

Velociúsne sagitta Romanis volat

Excussa nervis? Turbine an metam petit

Graviore jaculum Romulâ intortum manu?

Quæ comparare regio se ausit Africæ,

Seu bello onustos in acie elephantas regat,

Seu docili anhelos indole sonipedes domet,

Equitémque doceat pariter & frænos pati?

Hâc arte, princeps, Roma non Zamam anteit.

JUBA.

Vis ossium illa est atque nervorum : altiùs

Romanus aciem mentis intendit suæ.

Humanitatis scilicet studio feros

Formare

A Roman foul is bent on higher views ;

To civilize the rude unpolifh'd world,

To lay it under the reftraint of laws,

To make man mild, and fociable to man,

To cultivate the wild licentious favage

With wifdom, difcipline, and lib'ral arts,

Th' embellifhments of life.   Virtues like thefe

Make human nature fhine, reform the foul,

And break our fierce barbarians into men.

SYPHAX.

Patience, kind heav'ns! Excufe an old man's warmth

What are thefe wond'rous civilizing arts,

This Roman polifh, and this fmooth behaviour,

That render man thus tractable and tame ?

Are they not only to difguife our paffions,

To fet our looks at variance with our thoughts,

To check the ftarts and fallies of the foul,

And break off all its commerce with the tongue ?

JUBA.

Formare cultus hominum, inhofpitos facris

Frænare populos legibus, & icto rudes

Sociare gentes fœdere : hæc virtus, Syphax,

Romana pulchris artibus vitam excolit,

Placidófque mores barbarum mundum docet.

SYPHAX.

Quæ, quæfo, Romana ifta, quæ tandem fuit

Jactata virtus ? Quippe mendaci docet

Simulare vultu fenfa, fpeciofo oblita

Dare verba fuco, fimul alia premere finu,

Simul alia loqui, omnem abrogans linguæ fidem,

Quam fraudis infcia cordis humani dedit

Interpretem natura.

E 3   JUBA.

JUBA.

To ſtrike thee dumb, turn up thy eyes to *Cato*.
There may'ſt thou ſee to what a godlike height
The Roman virtues lift up mortal man,
While good, and juſt, and anxious for his friends,
He's ſtill ſeverely bent againſt himſelf.
Renouncing ſleep, and reſt, and food, and eaſe,
He ſtrives with thirſt and hunger, toil and heat;
And when his fortune ſets before him all
The pomps and pleaſures, that his ſoul can wiſh,
His rigid virtue will accept of none.

SYPHAX.

Believe me, prince, there's not an African,
That traverſes our vaſt Numidian deſerts,
In queſt of prey, and lives upon his bow,
But better practiſes theſe boaſted virtues.
Coarſe are his meals, the fortune of the chaſe;
Amidſt the running ſtream he ſlakes his thirſt,
Toils all the day, and at th' approach of night

On

JUBA.

Non imitabilem .

Sufpice Catonem, quem extulit diis propè parem
Romana virtus. Sobrius, juftus, bonus,
Patiens laborum, frigoris, inediæ, fitis,
Conftans amicis, fibi feverus, omnia
Oblata blandæ dóna fortunæ abnuit.

SYPHAX.

Deferta Libyæ nemo noftratûm, Juba,
Venando luftrat, vitam & arcu fuftinet,
Qui non feveriùs hafce virtutes colit.
Curis folutus libero vaftos pede
Saltus pererrat, callidus tantùm feris
Struxiffe fraudes. Rivus extinguit fitim,
Fortuita fylvis præda venanti dapes.
Faciles miniftrat. Nox ubi diurno opprimit
Labore feffum, membra profternit folo ;
Recline durâ rupe fuftentat caput,
Levefque fomnos æthere fub udo trahit.

Deia

On the firſt friendly bank he throws him down,

Or reſts his head upon a rock 'till morn :

Then riſes freſh, purſues his wonted game,

And if the following day he chance to find

A new repaſt, or an untaſted ſpring,

Bleſſes his ſtars, and thinks it luxury.

JUBA.

Thy prejudices, Syphax, won't diſcern

What virtues grow from ignorance and choice,

Nor how the hero differs from the brute.

But grant, that others could with equal glory

Look down on pleaſures, and the baits of ſenſe ;

Where ſhall we find the man that bears affliction,

Great and majeſtic in his griefs, like *Cato ?*

Heav'ns ! with what ſtrength, what ſteadineſs of mind,

He triumphs in the midſt of all his ſuff'rings !

How does he riſe againſt a load of woes,

And thank the gods, that throw their weight upon him !

SYPHAX.

Dein cum recenti fole-fe recens levat,

Studia diurna fequitur, & fi venam aquæ

Fors reperit illibatam & intaĉtas dapes,

Superos adorat, féque regifico frui

Luxu arbitratur.

JUBA.

Barbaro abreptus, Syphax,

Furore nefcis, vir quid interfit viro,

Vel quid humile fupra vulgus heroem levet.

Sed efto: molles alter illecebras pari

Virtute fpernat: Mente quis adeò tamen

Animofus atque fortis adverfæ ferat

Sortis ruinam ? Quippe quò premitur magis,

Hoc fortiore ftat inter ærumnas gradu,

Malífque ab ipfis robur affumit novum.

SYPHAX.

'Tis pride, rank pride, and haughtinefs of foul ;
I think the Romans call it ftoicifm.
Had not your royal father thought fo highly
Of Roman virtue, and of *Cato*'s caufe,
He had not fall'n by a flave's hand, inglorious :
Nor would his flaughter'd army now have lain
On Afric fands, disfigured with their wounds,
To gorge the wolves and vultures of Numidia.

JUBA.

Why didft thou call my forrows up afrefh ?
My father's name brings tears into my eyes.

SYPHAX.

Oh, that you'd profit by your father's ills !

JUBA.

What wouldft thou have me do ?

SYPHAX.

Abandon *Cato*.

JUBA.

SYPHAX.

Id infolentis arguit faftum viri :

Ni fallor, Itali Stoicum faftum vocant.

Romanæ opinio tanta virtutis nifi

Fidum Catoni tuum ita junxiffet patrem,

Acerba non fic fata fervili manu

Inglorius obiiffet; inhumata Libycis

Non tot virorum millia jacerent agris,

Paftura rabidos vulturum & lupûm greges.

JUBA.

Renovare triftem quid, Syphax, luctum jubes ?

Cùm reputo patrem ægro dolore cor tumet,

Lachrymìfque manare humidæ incipiunt genæ.

SYPHAX.

O fi paternis fapere didiciffes malis !

JUBA.

Age fare, quonam fapere me velis modo ?

SYPHAX.

Defere Catonem.

JUBA.

JUBA.

Syphax, I fhould be more than twice an orphan
By fuch a lofs.

SYPHAX.

Ay, there's the tie that binds you!
You long to call him father. Marcia's charms
Work in your heart unfeen, and plead for *Cato*.
No wonder you are deaf to all I fay.

JUBA.

Syphax, ycur zeal becomes importunate.
I've hitherto permitted it to rave,
And talk at large; but learn to keep it in,
Left it fhould take more freedom than I'll give it.
But *Cato* never at a time like this*
Would lay out his great foul in words, and wafte
Such precious moments. No! his life's at ftake;
And warm with flaughter, our victorious foe
Threat'ns aloud and calls me to the field.

* Thefe five verfes are *nearly* taken out of the fifth fcene of
the firft act.

SYPHAX.

JUBA.

Sic patre bis orbus forem.

SYPHAX.

Hoc nempe rebar vinculo obftringi Jubam.
Marcia Catonem blanda commendat patrem.
Nil miror equidem fi aure tam furdâ accipis
Monita, fi ita tibi dicta vilefcunt mea.

JUBA.

Syphax. caveto : liberas linguæ hactenus
Permifi habenas : difce dehinc premere tamen,
Ne plus loquare, audire quám reges decet.
Sed otiofa terere caufando pudet
Tempora, Catonis dubia dum pendet falus,
Dum marte flagrans Cæfar in aciem vocat.

SYPHAX.

SYPHAX Solus.

Ten thoufand curfes light on thee and *Cato !*

END OF THE FIRST ACT.

ACT

SYPHAX Solus.

Nigrantis erebi mille dii perdant malis

Jubam & Catonem! .... Caſſus in ventum hactenus

Labor omnis iit. At cardine haud tanto decet

Ceſſare rerum. Sunt mihi modi, ſunt doli,

Sunt technæ & artes mille. Tentabo omnia,

Quò pervicax frangatur ingenium Jubæ.

FINIS ACTUS PRIMI.

ACTUS

A C T II.

SCENE I.

SEMPRONIUS, LUCIUS, PORCIUS, SENATORES.

SEMPRONIUS.

ROME ſtill ſurvives in this aſſembled ſenate.
Let us remember, we are *Cato's* friends,
And act like men, who claim that glorious title.

LUCIUS.

Cato will ſoon be here and open to us
Th' occaſion of our meeting.　Hark! he comes.
　　　　　　　　　　　[*A ſound of trumpets.*
May all the guardian gods of Rome direct him!

　　　　　　　　　　　　　　　ENTER

ACTUS SECUNDUS.

SCENA PRIMA.

SEMPRONIUS, LUCIUS, PORCIUS, Senators.

SEMPRONIUS.

HOC in fenatu Roma nunc etiam viget.

Nos cum Catone retrò ruentis imperî

Fortuna junxit. Noftra fibi conftet fides :

Sumamus animos grandibus cæptis pares,

Româque dignos.

LUCIUS.

Ipfe mox aderit *Cato,*

Noftríque præfens confilî aperiet modum.

[*Tuba canit.*

Audin ? adeffe nunciat tubæ canor.

Dii fofpitales, Roma queis curæ fuit,

Cœleftem amico numine affervent virum !

INTRAT

ENTER CATO.

CATO.

Fathers, we once again are met in council.
Cæfar's approach has fummon'd us together,
And Rome attends her fate from our refolves.
How fhall we treat this bold afpiring man ?
Succefs ftill follows him, and backs his crimes.
Pharfalia gave him Rome, Egypt has fince
Receiv'd his yoke, and the whole Nile is Cæfar's.
Why fhould I mention Juba's overthrow,
And Scipio's death ? Numidia's burning fands
Still fmoke with blood. 'Tis time we fhould decree,
What courfe to take. Our foe advances on us,
And envies us even Lybia's fultry deferts.
Fathers, pronounce your thoughts. Are they ftill fixt
To hold it out, and fight it to the laft ?
Or are your hearts fubdu'd at length, and wrought
By time, and ill fuccefs to a fubmiffion ?
Sempronius, fpeak.

SEMPRONIUS,

INTRAT CATO.

CATO.

Patriæ labantis fata, libertas, falus

Confilia veftra petere me cogit, Patres.

Lachrymofa portans bella propiori impetu

Minatur hoftis. Infolens viri furor

Quâ reprimetur? Scelera perficere improbus

Pergit, nec ufquam fcelera fucceffu carent.

Pharfalica acies Cæfari Romam dedit,

Quaffata deinceps corruit Memphis folo,

Jugumque totâ Nilus Ægypto fubit.

Quid Scipionis fata, quid cladem Jubæ

Memorem? Æftuanti fanguine etiamnum calent

Lybies arenæ. Rapidus hoftis ingruit,

Et ipfa vel deferta nobis invidet

Arentis Africæ. Agite nunc ergo, Patres,

Quid cuique fieri placeat, in medium date:

Malifne victos cedere tyranno juvet,

An fortiter pro patriâ, Româ atque Diis

Ad ultimum certare. Semproni, incipe.

SEMPRONIUS.

SEMPRONIUS.

My voice is ſtill for war.

Gods ! can a Roman ſenate long debate,

Which of the two to chooſe, ſlav'ry or death ?

No, let us riſe at once, gird on our ſwords,

And at the head of our remaining troops,

Attack the foe, break through the thick array

Of his throng'd legions, and charge home upon him.

Perhaps ſome arm, more lucky than the reſt,

May reach his heart, and free the world from bondage.

Riſe, fathers, riſe : 'tis Rome demands your help.

Riſe, and revenge her ſlaughter'd citizens,

Or ſhare their fate. The corps of half her ſenate

Manure the fields of Theſſaly, while we

Sit here delib'rating in cold debates,

If we ſhould ſacrifice our lives to honour,

Or wear them out in ſervitude and chains.

Rouſe up for ſhame ! Our brothers of Pharſalia

Point

SEMPRONIUS.

Quifquamne claro genere Romanus poteft
Pendere dubius, utrûmne præponat necem,
An fervitutem? Bella, mavortia geri
Bella placet. Adeò protinus eamus, Patres,
Ferróque latera vindice accinéti improbum
Petamus hoftem. Mille denfatis licèt
Cuneis virorum robora tyrannum tegant,
Rumpemus aditus. Quis fcit, an reliquis magis
Profpera tot inter una tranfadigat virum .
Hafta, patriamque liberet & orbem jugo?
Quin furgite, Patres. Roma, libertas vocant.
Surgite jacentûm civium ulturi neces,
Similíve fato fimile merituri decus.
Sanguine patricio Theffali exundant agri,
Nòfque dubitando trahimus hîc lenti diem,
Pulchramne præftet petere per mortem decus,
An luétuofum ferre fervitii probrum.
Torpentium animorum fitum excutiat pudor.
Pharfalicâ cæforum acie oberrant ducum

Manes

Point at their wounds, and cry aloud .... To battl

Great Pompey's fhade complains, that we are flow,

And Scipio's ghoft walks unreveng'd amongft us.

CATO.

Let not a torrent of impetuous zeal

Tranfport thee thus beyond the bounds of reafon.

True fortitude is feen in great exploits,

That juftice warrants, and that wifdom guides.

All elfe is tow'ring frenzy and diftraction.

Are not the lives of thofe, who draw the fword

In Rome's defence, intrufted to our care?

Should we thus lead them to a field of flaughter,

Might not th' impartial world with reafon fay,

We lavifh'd at our deaths the blood of thoufands,

To grace our fall, and make our ruin glorious?

Lucius, we next would know, what's your opinion.

LUCIUS.

Manes inulti : vulnera oftentant fua,

Et nos ad arma voce lugubri vocant

Ad arma, Patres. Magnus en ! moræ reos

Pompeius urget. Sibi parentandum inferas

Clamat per umbras Scipio.

CATO.

Mentem cave,

Ne fortè rapiat nimius armorum furor.

Nifi ratione nixa ftet, virtus migrat

In temeritatem. Publicæ quicquid rei

Fortuna reliqui fecit, eft noftræ, Patres,

Curæ repoftum. Hiantia patriæ decet

Curare vulnera, non novis vetera malis

Exafperare. Prodigi vitæ nimis

Meritò arguemur, fi tot illuftres viros,

Ut noftra decorent funera, in medias neces

Projicimus. At quæ nunc tibi, Luci, fedet

Sententia, audire libet.

LUCIUS.

My thoughts, I muſt confeſs, are turn'd on peace.

Already have our quarrels fill'd the world

With widows, and with orphans. Scythia mourns

Our guilty wars, and earth's remoteſt regions

Lie half unpeopled by the feuds of Rome.

'Tis time to ſheath the ſword, and ſpare mankind.

It is not Cæſar, but the gods, my fathers,

The gods declare againſt us, and repel

Our vain attempts.   To urge the foe to battle,

Prompted by blind revenge and wild deſpair,

Were to refuſe th' awards of providence,

And-not to reſt in heav'n's determination.

Already have we ſhewn our love to Rome,

Now let us ſhew ſubmiſſion to the gods.

We took up arms, not to revenge ourſelves,

But free the commonwealth.   When this end fails,

Arms have no further uſe.   Our country's cauſe,

That drew our ſwords, now wreſts 'em from our hand

And bids us not delight in Roman blood,

                                        Unprofitably

LUCIUS.

Eft fufum fatis

Supérque fanguinis.   Impio bello nimis

Quaffatus orbis vix fuas clades capit.

Nulla regio ufquam eft, five quà Titan levat,

Seu quà remoto mergit oceano diem,

Quam non replerit fanguine Aufonium nefas.

Romana latè bella deplorat viris

Viduata Scythia, & mundus oppofito procul

Sub axe, noftro marte populatus jacet.

Cruenta tempus tela vaginis tegi,

Generíque tandem parcere humano jubet.

Non noftra Cæfar aufa contundit, Patres,

Sed vis deorum.   Numine adverfo irrita

Quid gerimus ultrà bella ?   Cedamus Jovi.

Ubi caufa belli ceffat, & ceffet furor.

Patriæ atque libertatis amor arma ad pia

Nos excitavit.   Quicquid in manu fuit,

Fecimus abundè. .Gloriæ eft factum fatis,

Fortè nimis iræ, patriæ certè parum.

F   Si

Unprofitably fhed. What men could do,

Is done already. Heav'n and earth will witnefs,

If Rome muft fall, that we are innocent.

SEMPRONIUS.

This fmooth difcourfe, and mild behaviour oft

Conceal a traitor. Something whifpers me,

All is not right. *Cato*, beware of Lucius.

[*Afide to Cato.*

CATO.

Let us appear nor rafh nor diffident.

Immod'rate valour fwells into a fault,

And fear, admitted into public councils,

Betrays like treafon. Let us fhun 'em both.

Fathers, I cannot fee, that our affairs

Are grown thus defperate. We have bulwarks round us.

Within our walls are troops inured to toil

In Afric's heats, and feafon'd to the fun.

Numidia's fpacious kingdom lies behind us,

Ready to rife at its young prince's call.

While there is hope, do not diftruft the gods :

But

Si Roma denique cadit, atteſtor fidem
Hominum Deûmque, ſcelere non noſtro cadit.

SEMPRONIUS.

Se perduellis ſæpè quæſito tegit
Colore : vereor aliquis ut lateat dolus.

Cato, Lucio ne crede.   *Seorſim Catoni.*

CATO.

Degeneres timor
Animos coarguit, agit in præceps furor.
Medium occupemus tramitem.   Quidni benè
Sperare, Patres, rebus etiamnum licet ?
Dum noſtra fortes latera tot cingunt viri,
Sueti labores martis & ſolem pati,
Quorſum proboſo colla ſubdemus jugo ?
Numidia gentes aperit immenſas, Jubæ
Facere paratas juſſa.   Dum ſpes eſt ſuper,
Stat fidere Jovi.   Ne ante præfixum diem
Cadat alta Roma.   Liberis donec licet,

Deûm

But wait at leaſt 'till Cæſar's near approach

Force us to yield.   'Twill never be too late

To ſue for chains, and own a conqueror.

Why ſhould Rome fall a moment ere her time ?

No, let us draw her term of freedom out

In its full length, and ſpin it to the laſt.

So ſhall we gain ſtill one day's liberty,

And let me periſh.   But in *Cato*'s judgment,

A day, an hour of virtuous liberty,

Is worth a whole eternity in bondage.

ENTER MARCUS.

MARCUS.

Fathers, this moment, as I watch'd the gate,

Lodg'd on my poſt, a herald is arriv'd

From Cæſar's camp, and with him comes old Decius,

The Roman knight.   He carries in his looks

Impatience, and demands to ſpeak with *Cato.*

CATO.

By permiſſion, fathers, bid him enter.

[*Exit Marcus.*

Deûm fruamur munere : ubi fummum venit

Fatum, licebit vincla victoris pati.

Hâc luce mallet, imo & hâc horâ *Cato*

Oppetere liber, quàm jugo oppreffus dies

Ducere perennes.

INTRAT MARCUS.

MARCUS.

Quà arva profpectat, mihi

Commiffa porta, à Cæfare advenit citus

Modò fecialis : venit & Decius eques

Romanus. Aliquid ferre fe magni indicat,

Tuófque, genitor, illicò affatus petit.

CATO.

Succedere jube. Decius hic olim mihi

[*Exit Marcus.*

F 3   Fuerat

Decius was once my friend, but other profpects

Have loos'd thofe ties, and bound him faft to Cæfar.

SCENE

Fuerat amicus. Alia tranfverfum dehinc

Studia abftulêre, & Cæfari focium impiis

Junxêre in armis.

SCENA

SCENE II.

DECIUS, CATO.

DECIUS.

CÆSAR fends health to *Cato*.

CATO.

             Could he fend it
To *Cato*'s flaughter'd friends, it would be welcome.
Are not your orders to addrefs the fenate ?

DECIUS.

   My bufinefs is with *Cato*.   Cæfar fees
The ftraits to which you're driven ; and, as he knows
Cato's high worth, is anxious for your life.

CATO.

SCENA SECUNDA.

DECIUS, CATO.

DECIUS.

PLURIMAM, *Cato,* tibi
Cæfar falutem.

CATO.

Si mittere occifis modò
Poffet & amicis, grata mihi falus foret.
Edenda fi quæ porrò mandata afferas,
Coram, en fenatus.

DECIUS.

Res mihi tecum, *Cato.*
Ad quas redigere anguftias, Cæfar videt.
Et nota quoniam merita permagni æftimat,
Tuæ falutis anxias curas fovet.

F 5 *CATO.*

CATO.

My life is grafted on the fate of Rome.

Would he fave *Cato* ?   Bid him fpare his country.

Tell your dictator this : and tell him, *Cato*

Difdains a life, which he has power to offer.

DECIUS.

Rome and her fenators fubmit to Cæfar.

Her generals and her confuls are no more,

Who check'd his conquefts, and deny'd his triumphs.

Why will not *Cato* be this Cæfar's friend ?

CATO.

Thofe very reafons you have urged, forbid it.

DECIUS.

Cato, I've orders to expoftulate,

And reafon with you, as from friend to friend.

Think on the ftorm, that gathers o'er your head,

And threatens ev'ry hour to burft upon it.

Still may you ftand high in your country's honours,

Do but comply, and make your peace with Cæfar.

Rome

CATO.

Romæ salute nixa mea pendet salus.

Mihi parcere velit ? Patriæ parcat suæ.

I, castra repete, & principi hæc refer tuo :

Accipere vitam renuit indignans *Cato,*

Quam Cæsar offert.

DECIUS.

Cæsari subdit caput

Roma & senatus. Consulum imperium fuit.

Quotquot triumphis Cæsaris & armis duces

Contrà obstitêre, pulvere immixti jacent.

Age ergo, victoris sequere tu quoque fidem.

CATO.

Illa ipsa, quæ mihi facta commemoras, vetant.

DECIUS.

Per nomen ego te sacrum amicitiæ rogo,

Qualis procella vertici immineat, vide.

A Cæsare secundum orbis aspiciet suum

Pronus Catonem, laude tergeminâ ad deos ·

Roma

Rome will rejoice, and caft its eyes on *Cato*,

As on the Second of mankind.

CATO.

No more.

I muft not think of life on fuch conditions.

DECIUS.

Cæfar is well acquainted with your virtues,

And therefore fets this value on your life.

Let him but know the price of *Cato*'s friendfhip,

And name your terms.

CATO.

Bid him difband his legions,

Reftore the commonwealth to liberty,

Submit his actions to the public cenfure,

And ftand the judgment of a Roman fenate.

Let him do this, and *Cato* is his friend.

DECIUS.

Cato, the world talks loudly of your wifdom....

CATO.

Roma ipfa tollet, pace fi faꞔâ modò
Agnofcere æqui jura viꞔoris lubet.

CATO.

Ne plura : vitam hoc munere pacifci nefas.

DECIUS.

Effare, quâ tua tandem amicitia queat
Mercede redimi, renuet & Cæfar nihil,
Quo tale palmis priftinis addat decus.

CATO.

Exercitum dimittat ; exolvat jugo
Romam, Qairitum libero arbitrio & Patrum
Dijudicanda faꞔa permittat fua.
Hâc poterit unâ lege fibi Cæfar fidem
Catonis emere.

DECIUS.

Fama non levis tuæ eft
Sapientiæ, *Cato.*

CATO.

CATO.

Nay more, tho' *Cato*'s voice was ne'er employed
To clear the guilty, and to varnifh crimes,
Myfelf will mount the Roftrum in his favour,
And ftrive to gain his pardon from the people.

DECIUS.

A ftile, like this, becomes a conqueror.

CATO.

Decius, a ftile, like this, becomes a Roman.

DECIUS.

What is a Roman, that is Cæfar's foe ?

CATO.

Greater than Cæfar: he's a friend to virtue.

DECIUS.

Confider, *Cato*, you're in Utica,
And at the head of your own little fenate.

You

CATO.

Imò vox quanquam mea

Verſata nunquam in publicis cauſis fuit,

Neque ſuevit excuſare commiſſum ſcelus,

Orator ipſe roſtra conſcendam tamen,

Veniámque ſupplex Cæſari à populo petam.

DECIUS.

Cato, hic ferocem ſermo victorem decet.

CATO.

Juſti tenacem hic ſermo Romanum decet.

DECIUS.

Romanus ille qualis aut quantus fuit,

Cæſari inimicus ?

CATO.

Major ipſo Cæſare :

Eſt ille amicus nempe virtuti & Deo.

DECIUS.

Quis ſis, Cato, vel unde compulſus, vide.

Non nunc frequentium inter applauſus Patrum

Celſa

You don't now thunder in the capitol,

With all the mouths of Rome to fecond you.

CATO.

Let him confider that, who drives us hither.

'Tis Cæfar's fword has made Rome's fenate little,

And thinn'd its ranks. Alas, thy dazzled eye

Beholds this man in a falfe glaring light,

Which conqueft and fuccefs have thrown upon him.

Did'ft thou but view him right, thou'dft fee him black

With murder, treafon, facrilege, and crimes,

That ftrike my foul with horror but to name 'em.

I know thou look'ft on me, as on a wretch

Befet with ills, and cover'd with misfortunes.

But, by the gods I fwear, millions of worlds

Should never buy me to be like that Cæfar.

DECIUS.

Does *Cato* fend this anfwer back to Cæfar,

For all his gen'rous cares, and proffer'd friendfhip?

CATO.

Celsa capitolia voce fulmineâ quatis.

Inclusus Uticâ fine spe & auxilio jaces.

CATO.

Hoc ille potiùs cogitet, qui nos eò

Angustiarum compulit. Tenuem, ut vides,

Romæ senatum Cæsaris fecit scelus.

Mihi crede, falsum est lumen & inanis rei

Splendentis umbra, quâ ille vir adeò tibi

Fulgere videtur. Spissa si ab oculis foret

Remota nubes, sanguine, rapinis, dolo

Totum inquinatum cerneres. Miserum, scio,

Me spernis, ærumnosum & afflictum malis.

Sed per Tonantem juro, priùs omnis mihi

Oblatus orbis cum omnibus regnis ruat,

Quàm Cæsar esse, forte mutatâ, velim.

DECIUS.

Hæccine referri Cæsari *Cato* jubet

Responsa? Studiis hanccine rependit vicem?

CATO.

CATO.

His cares for me are infolent and vain.
Prefumptuous man ! The gods take care of *Cato.*
Would Cæfar fhew the greatnefs of his foul ?
Bid him employ his care for thefe my friends,
And make good ufe of his ill-gotten pow'r,
By fhelt'ring men much better than himfelf.

DECIUS.

Your high unconquer'd heart makes you forget
You are a man. You rufh on your deftruction.
But I have done. When I relate hereafter
The tale of this unhappy embaffy,
All Rome will be in tears.

[*Exit Decius.*

SCENE

CATO.

Sunt Cæfaris vana ftudia. Indignor viri
Curam infolentem. Eft fcilicet penes deos
Salus Catonis. Si tamen Cæfar cupit
Clemens videri, opibus malè paratis meos
Juvet hos amicos : fi fuæ mentis cupit
Excelfitatem oftendere, hos fervet viros
Se juftiores.

DECIUS.

Ifta vis animi, *Cato*,
Nimis infolens te tollit oblitum tui.
Prudens fciénfque certum in exitium ruis.
Legatione fed ego fum functus meâ.
Notus ubi fuerit exitus, totam dolor
Invadet urbem.

[*Exit Decius.*

SCENA

SCENE III.

SEMPRONIUS, LUCIUS, CATO, SENATORS.

SEMPRONIUS.

CATO, we thank thee.
The mighty genius of immortal Rome
Speaks in thy voice; thy foul breathes liberty.
Cæfar will fhrink to hear the words thou utter'ft,
And fhudder in the midft of all his conquefts.

LUCIUS.

The fenate owns its gratitude to *Cato,*
Who with fo great a foul confults its fafety,
And guards our lives, while he neglects his own.

SEMPRONIUS.

Sempronius gives no thanks on this account.
Lucius feems fond of life. When liberty is gone,
Life grows infipid, and has loft its relifh.

O could

SCENA TERTIA.

SEMPRONIUS, LUCIUS, CATO, Senatores.

SEMPRONIUS.

FERRE quas grates parem ?

Te, *Cato*, loquente, eſt viſa libertas loqui

Geniûſque Romæ.   Scelera meditantem nova

Vox iſta reprimet Cæſarem, aut ſternet metu.

LUCIUS.

Uno ſenatus omnis aſſenſu refert

Grates Catoni, publicæ dum ſic vigil

Cavet ſaluti, providus parum ſuæ.

SEMPRONIUS.

Amor tuendæ Lucium vitæ tenet.

Sed vita quid juvat, ubi libertas perit ?

Me potiùs adigat fulmine ſub umbras Pater,

Pallentis umbras tartari & noctis chaos,

Quàm

O could my dying hand but lodge a ſword
In Cæſar's boſom, and revenge my country,
By heav'ns I could enjoy the pangs of death,
And ſmile in agony.

LUCIUS.

Others, perhaps,
May ſerve their country with as warm a zeal,
Tho' 'tis not kindled into ſo much rage.

SEMPRONIUS.

This ſober conduct is a mighty virtue
In lukewarm patriots.   But what is life ?
'Tis not to ſtalk about, and draw freſh air
From time to time, or gaze upon the ſun ;
'Tis to be free.

CATO.

Come, no more, Sempronius.
All here are friends to Rome, and to each other.
Let us not weaken ſtill the weaker ſide
By our diviſions.

SEMPRONIUS.

Quàm videam iniquo fubditos cives jugo.

Stet, me cadente, falva libertas modò,

Mortes per omnes placidus hanc animam dabo.

LUCIUS.

Fortè haud minori pectus hoc ftudio flagrat

Defendere patriam, æftuat quanquam minùs

Furore turbidum. .

SEMPRONIUS.

Ifta moderatio virum,

Cui vivere eft dulce, juvet.   At vivere quid eft ?

Non huc & huc curfare, non auras novas

Subinde trahere, aut folis afpicere jubar ;

Eft effe liberum.

CATO.

Ira ne difcors agat

Privata in odia, Roma quos fibi mutuo

Amore junxit.   Pace concordi vigent

Res parvæ, câdem maximæ abruptâ ruunt.

SEMPRONIUS.

SEMPRONIUS.

Cato, my refentments
Are facrificed to Rome.   I ftand reprov'd.

CATO.

Fathers, 'tis time you come to a refolve.

LUCIUS.

Cato, we all go into your opinion.
Cæfar's behaviour has convinced the fenate,
We ought to hold it out, 'till terms arrive.

SEMPRONIUS.

We ought to hold it out till death.   But *Cato*,
My private voice is drown'd amid the fenate's.

CATO.

Then let us rife, my friends, and ftrive to fill
This little interval, this paufe of life,
While yet our liberty and fates are doubtful,
With refolution, friendfhip, Roman bravery,
And all the virtues we can crowd into it,

That

SEMPRONIUS.

En me paratum quicquid aut facere aut pati,
Ubi *Cato* jusserit.

CATO.

Hora consiliis moram
Præcidere monet.

LUCIUS.

Ipse quod censet *Cato*,
Id censet & senatus.   Usque dum bonis
Pax legibus conveniat, audendum reor.

SEMPRONIUS.

Est dimicandum, quamdiu vita est super.

CATO.

Surgamus ergo, dúmque libertas, salus,
Et fata nutant dubia, justitiâ, fide,
Officio & omni genere virtutum brevis
Certemus ævi, tandem ut invidiâ deûm
Si sit cadendum, morte generosâ inclytos

G   Nos

That heav'n may fay, it ought to be prolong'd.

                    [*Exeunt fenators.*

SCENE

Nos longiorem grata posteritas canat
Meruisse vitam.

[Exeunt senatores.

G 2 SCENA

SCENE IV.

CATO, JUBA.

CATO.

JUBA, the Roman fenate has refolv'd,
'Till time give better profpects, ftill to keep
The fword unfheath'd, and turn its edge on Cæfar.

JUBA.

The refolution fits a Roman fenate.
But *Cato*, lend me for a while thy patience,
And condefcend to hear a young man fpeak.
My father, when fome days before his death
He order'd me to march for Utica,
Alas, I thought not then his death fo near,
Wept o'er me, preft me in his aged arms,
And, as his griefs gave way, my fon, faid he,
Whatever fortune fhall befal thy father,

SCENA QUARTA.

CATO, JUBA.

CATO.

$\mathbb{P}$ATRIBUS eft ratùm, Juba,
Forti repellere Cæfarem & bellum manu.

JUBA.

Sententia patres ifta Romanos decet.
Dignare tu quoque pauca memorantem Jubam
Audire. Paucos genitor ante obitum dies,
Haud rebar equidem mortem ita propinquam viro
Tunc imminere, quando me juffit Uticam
Tendere, trementes fuftulit in ulnas fenex
Blandè ofculatus, multa collachrymans. Dolor
Ut primus abiit, quicquid eveniat mihi,
Nate, inquit, efto Catoni amicus. Aufpice

G 3 Surges

Be *Cato*'s friend. He'll train thee up to great
And virtuous deeds. Do but obferve him well,
Thou'lt fhun misfortunes, or thou'lt learn to bear 'em.

CATO.

Juba, thy father was a worthy prince,
And merited, alas, a better fate.
But heav'n thought otherwife.

JUBA.

My father's fate
In fpite of all the fortitude, that fhines
Before my face in *Cato*'s great example,
Subdues my foul, and fills my eyes with tears.

CATO.

It is an honeft forrow, and becomes thee.

JUBA.

My father drew refpect from foreign climes.
The kings of Afric fought him for their friend;
Kings far remote, that rule, as fame reports,
Behind the hidden fources of the Nile,

In

Surges Catone ad omne virtutum decus.

Illo duce, fugies mala aut difces pati.

CATO.

Tuus ille fummâ laude cumulatus pater

Meliora fuerat fata commeritus, Juba.

Diis aliter eft vifum.

JUBA.

Ubi patris imago fubit,

Lachrymis madefcunt me vel invito genæ.

Omnis animo virtus abit, fuperat dolor.

CATO.

Honeftus eft ille dolor, & dignus Jubâ.

JUBA.

Gentes remotas fama complevit patris.

Hunc pace bellóque Africæ reges fibi

Socium ambiebant,   Maurus & vultum niger

Getulus Æthiópfque, quíque ultrà jacent

Nili receffus, quíque, ut eft fama, incolunt

G 4   Alio

In diſtant worlds, on t'other ſide the ſun.

Oft have their black ambaſſadors appeared

Loaden with gifts, and fill'd the courts of Zama.

CATO.

I am no ſtranger to thy father's greatneſs.

JUBA.

I would not boaſt the greatneſs of my father,

But point ont new alliances to Cato.

Had we not better leave this Utica,

To arm Numidia in our cauſe, and court

Th' aſſiſtance of my father's pow'rful friends?

Did they know Cato, our remoteſt kings

Would pour embattled multitudes about him.

Their ſwarthy hoſts would darken all our plains,

Doubling the native horror of the war,

And making death more grim.

CATO.

Alio calentes fole trans Gangem plagas,

Donis onufti petere amicitiam & opem

Venêre Zamam.

CATO.

Gloria mihi haud eft tui

Ignota patris.

JUBA.

Patris amicitias tibi

Dum commemoro, non patrium jacto decus ;

Jungenda fœdera tibi nova monftro, nova

Subfidia belli. Nunquid hanc præftat Uticam

Deferere, & omni Numidiâ armatâ, fimul

In focietatem fœderis amicos patris

Excire reges ? Cognitum fi orbi foret,

Virtute & armis quantus incedas, Cato,

Totam videres Africam è gremio nigros

Populos vomentem ad figna confluere tua,

Sociáfque bello latè inhorrentes novo

Fervefcere acies.

CATO.

And can'ſt thou think

Cato will fly before the ſword of Cæſar,

Reduced like Hannibal to ſeek relief

From court to court, and wander up and down

A vagabond in Afric ?

JUBA.

Cato, perhaps,

I'm too officious ; but my forward cares

Would fain preſerve a life of ſo much value.

My heart is wounded, when I ſee ſuch virtue

Afflicted by the weight of ſuch misfortunes.

CATO.

Thy noblenefs of foul obliges me.

But know, young prince, that valour ſoars above

What the world calls misfortune and affliction.

Theſe are not ills ; elfe would they never fall

On heav'n's firſt fav'rites, and the beſt of men.

The gods, in bounty, work up ſtorms about us,

That give mankind occaſion to exert

Their

CATO.

Cæfari an timidum putas
Cedere Catonem velle ? Me, ut vagus Hannibal,
Libycas per urbes fupplicem & regum hofpitem
Auxilia petere ?

JUBA.

Forfan officio tibi
Peccare nimio videor, anxius tuæ
Dum ftudeo vitæ, & fuggero auxilium malis.

CATO.

Eft tua mihi accepta pietas.   Noris tamen,
Juba ; quæ imperitum vulgus appellat mala,
Adverfa fortuna, dolor, ærumnæ, mala
Cenfenda non funt, forte cùm æquali accidunt
Bonis malífque.   His altior cœlum petit
Generofus animus.   Afperis fatis pios
Exercet aliquando deus, ut clara emicet
Magis inde virtus, quæ nifi rerum arduo

Spendefcat

Their hidden ftrength, and throw out into practice
Virtues, which fhun the day, and lie concealed
In the fmooth feafons and the calms of life.

JUBA.

I'm charm'd whene'er thou talk'ft. I pant for virtue,
And all my foul endeavours at perfection.

CATO.

Doft thou love watchings, abftinence, and toil,
Laborious virtues all? Learn them from *Cato*.
Succefs and fortune muft thou learn from Cæfar.

JUBA.

The beft good fortune, that can fall on Juba,
The whole fuccefs, at which my heart afpires,
Depends on *Cato*.

CATO.

What does Juba fay?
Thy words confound me.

JUBA.

I would fain retract them.
Give 'em me back again. They aim'd at nothing.

CATO.

Splendefcat ufu, tecta velut umbrâ diem
Lucémque fugit.

JUBA.

Ita dum loquere, totus, *Cato,*
Virtutem anhelus fpiro.

CATO.

Vigilias amas,
Æftum, laborem, frigus, & famem & fitim ?
Hæc ab Catone difce, fortunam ab aliis.

JUBA.

Felicitas, fortuna, & omnis fpes Jubæ
Te pendet uno.

CATO.

Verba quid volunt ?

JUBA.

Nihil :
Revocare liceat.

CATO.

CATO.

Tell me thy wifh, young prince; make not my ear
A ftranger to thy thoughts.

JUBA.

Oh, they're extravagant.
Still let me hide them.

CATO.

What can Juba afk,
That *Cato* will refufe?

JUBA.

I fear to name it.
Marcia inherits all her father's virtues.

CATO.

What wou'dſt thou fay?

JUBA.

Cato, thou haft a daughter.

CATO.

CATO.

Quod tuâ interfit, nihil

Cela Catonem.

JUBA.

Quæ modum excedunt, decet

Celare vota.

CATO.

Petere quid poteſt Juba,

Quod *Cato* recuſet ?

JUBA.

Eloqui vetat timor.

CATO.

Eloquere.

JUBA.

Dotes Marcia paternas habet.

CATO.

Quò verba ſpectant ?

JUBA.

Eſt tibi, *Cato*, filia.

CATO.

CATO.

Adieu, young prince.   I would not hear a word

Should leſſen thee in my eſteem.   Remember

The hand of fate is over us, and heav'n

Exacts ſeverity from all our thoughts.

It is not now a time to talk of aught

But chains, or conqueſt, liberty or death.

                                               [*Exit.*

                                                 SCENE

CATO.

Princeps valeto.　Quicquid imminuat tuam

Mihi, Juba, famam, audire nolim.　Dum premunt

Inimica fata, nos decet nihil, nisi

Vitam & triumphos, vincula aut mortem loqui.

[*Exit.*

SCENA

SCENE V.

SYPHAX, JUBA.

SYPHAX.

HOW's this, my prince! What, cover'd with
    confusion?
You look as if yon stern philosopher
Had just now chid you.

JUBA.

Syphax, I'm undone!

SYPHAX.

I know it well.

JUBA.

Cato thinks meanly of me.

SYPHAX.

And so will all mankind.

JUBA.

SCENA QUINTA.

SYPHAX, JUBA.

SYPHAX.

QUIS ille, Juba, quis ora fuffundit pudor ?
Quæ caufa luctûs ?

JUBA.

Heu, Syphax, perii mifer !

SYPHAX.

Hoc antè noram.

JUBA.

Me *Cato* vili æftimat.

SYPHAX.

Haud pluris orbis faciet.

JUBA.

JUBA.

I've opened to him
The weaknefs of my foul, my love for Marcia.

SYPHAX.

Cato's a proper perfon to entruft
A love-tale with.

JUBA.

Oh I could pierce my heart.
My foolifh heart ! Was ever wretch like Juba ?
Cato's difpleas'd, and Marcia loft for ever.

SYPHAX.

Young prince, I yet could give you good advice :
Marcia might ftill be your's.

JUBA.

What fay'ft thou, Syphax ?
By heav'ns thou turn'ft me all into attention.

SYPHAX.

Marcia might ftill be your's.

JUBA.

JUBA.

Aperui meos

Catoni amores.

SYPHAX.

Aptus eſt *Cato,* cui

Credas amores.

JUBA.

Solis ætherei jubar

Tædet tueri. Corde transfixo juvat

Occumbere umbris. Stulta quò miſerum abſtulit

Animi libido? Graviter heu! *Cato* mihi

Infenſus eſt; mihi Marcia æternùm perit.

SYPHAX.

Si quid monenti credis, etiamnum poteſt

Tua eſſe Marcia.

JUBA.

Quid loquere, Syphax?

SYPHAX.

Poteſt

Tua eſſe Marcia.

JUBA.

JUBA.

As how, dear Syphax ?

SYPHAX.

Juba commands Numidia's hardy troops,
Mounted on fteeds, unufed to the reftraint
Of curbs or bits, and fleeter than the winds.
Give but the word, we'll fnatch this damfel up,
And bear her off.

JUBA.

Can fuch difhoneft thoughts
Rife up in man ? Wouldft thou feduce my youth
To do an act, that would deftroy my honour ?

SYPHAX.

Gods, I could tear my beard to hear you talk !
Honour's a fine imaginary notion,
That draws in raw and unexperienc'd men
To real mifchiefs, while they hunt a fhadow.

JUBA.

JUBA.

Arte quâ poffit, doce.

SYPHAX.

Numidas feroces ducit ad bellum Juba,
Quos fræna ferre nefcii alipedes vehunt,
Prævertere Euros concitâ affueti fugâ.
Tu modò jubeto, virginémque hinc ociùs
Raptam avehemus.

JUBA.

Ore num potuit nefas
Excidere, probra quod nomini noftro allinat
Æterna.

SYPHAX.

Probra nomini! Nomen quid eft?
Inane fulgur nempe, fpeciofum nihil,
Aut fax cerebri fatua, quæ incautos trahit
Sæpè in malorum abrupta, dum errores vagæ
Sectantur umbræ.

JUBA.

JUBA.

Wouldſt thou degrade thy prince into a ruffian ?

SYPHAX.

The boaſted anceſtors of theſe great men,

Whoſe virtues you admire, were all ſuch ruffians.

This dread of nations, this almighty Rome,

That comprehends in her wide empire's bounds

All under heav'n, was founded on a rape.

Your Scipios, Cæſars, Pompeys, and your Catos,

Theſe gods on earth, are all the ſpurious brood

Of violated maids, of raviſh'd Sabines.

JUBA.

Syphax, I fear that hoary head of thine

Abounds too much in our Numidian wiles.

SYPHAX-

Indeed, my prince, you want to know the world.

JUBA.

JUBA.

Quid, tuo an fuades Jubæ

Agere latronem?

SYPHAX.

Quippe Romani patres,

Quos tu merere laudibus cœlum putas,

Tales fuêre.   Ille orbis edomiti pavor,

Superba Roma, Roma, quæ imperium mari

Terminat & aftris, virginum quondam fuit

Fundata raptu.   Scipio, Cæfar, *Cato*,

Pompeius, & quos Roma mortales deos

Dixit, Sabinis matribus referunt genus,

Spuria propago.

JUBA.

Vereor, ut, Syphax, tibi

Cerebrum Numidicis fit nimis fœtum dolis.

SYPHAX.

Mihi crede, mores tibi hominum noti parum.

H   *JUBA.*

JUBA.

If knowledge of the world makes man perfidious,
May Juba ever live in ignorance !

SYPHAX.

Go, go, you're young.

JUBA.

Gods, muft I tamely bear
This arrogance unanfwer'd ? Thou'rt a traitor,
A falfe old traitor.

SYPHAX.

I have gone too far.

[*Afide.*

JUBA.

Cato fhall know the bafenefs of thy foul.

SYPHAX.

Young prince, behold thefe locks, that are grown
white
Beneath a helmet in your father's battles.

JUBA.

JUBA.

Notitia at ista perfidos si homines facit,

O usque vitam ducat ignarus Juba.

SYPHAX.

Mihi apage sensa ista, puer : ætate indiges.

JUBA.

Dii ! siccine arrogantiam hanc lentus feram ?

False veterator, proditor patriæ es tuæ.

SYPHAX.

Me longiùs animi ardor incautum tulit.

[*Seorsim.*

JUBA.

Perfide latro, hæc tua *Cato* consilia sciet.

SYPHAX.

Viden' hos capillos ? Galeâ ut incincti albidum

Traxêre honorem, ductor & miles tui

Dum bella pugnabam patris !

JUBA.

JUBA.

Thofe locks fhall ne'er protect thy infolence.

SYPHAX.

Muft one rafh word, th' infirmity of age,
Throw down the merit of my better years ?
This the reward of a whole life of fervice !

[*Exit Juba.*

.... Curfe on the boy ! how fteadily he hears me.
I muft appeafe this ftorm, or perifh in it.

[*Exit Syphax.*

END OF THE SECOND ACT.

ACT

JUBA.

Mihi iste honor

Nusquam insolentiam teget.

SYPHAX.

Num ergo mihi

Vox una, vitium garrulæ ætatis leve,

Pristina laborum merita gestorum auferet?

[Exit Juba.

Styx mille pestes in caput pueri evomat!

Sed has oportet illicò procellæ minas

Placare, vel nos turbine effuso obruent.

[Exit Syphax.

FINIS ACTUS SECUNDI.

ACTUS

A C T III.

SCENE I.

SYPHAX, JUBA.

SYPHAX.

ALAS, my prince, how are you chang'd of late?*

I've known young Juba rife before the fun,

To beat the thicket where the tiger flept,

Or feek the lion in his dreadful haunts.

How did the colour mount into your cheeks,

When firft you rous'd him to the chace? I've feen you

Ev'n in the Libyan dog-days hunt him down,

---

* *Thefe verfes as far as lofe its fweetnefs, are taken from fcene V. act II.*

Then

ACTUS TERTIUS.

SCENA PRIMA.

SYPHAX, JUBA.

SYPHAX.

HEU qualis es quantúmque mutatus, Juba!

Heu quantùm ab illo degener pridem Jubâ,

Qui ftrata folitus linquere ante ortum diem,

Vel quando Sirius arva torrebat vapor,

Venando faltus atque fylvarum horrida

Dumeta obivit, five quâ rabida tigris,

Seu fulvus inter nemora dormivit leo?

Ardore quanto lumina micabas, ubi

Dejecta opacis præda decurrit jugis?

Clamore anhelo quantus urgebas fugam?

Then charge him clofe, provoke him to the rage

Of fangs and claws, and ftooping from your horfe

Rivet the panting favage to the ground.

JUBA.

Pr'ythee no more!

SYPHAX.

How would the old king fmile

To fee you weigh the paws, when tipp'd with gold,

And throw the fhaggy fpoils about your fhoulders.

JUBA.

Syphax, this old man's talk, tho' honey flow'd

From ev'ry word, would now lofe all its fweetnefs.

Te sæpè vidi cominùs lacessere

Leonis iras, unguium horribiles minas

Ultrò asperare, spiculo obtento truces

Excire morsus, móxque pronum ab equo arduos

Pendere in ictus, & reluctantem feram

Affigere solo.

JUBA.

Méne puerilis animi

Adeò esse rere, ut hisce condonem tua

Opprobria nugis?

SYPHAX.

Quanta longævi sinum

Regis replebant gaudia, ubi te auro graves

Attollere ungues vidit, & spolia humeros

Induere villis horrida!

JUBA.

Etiamsi fluant

Tibi verba melle, mihi modò invisa accident.

SYPHAX.

Sir, your great father never us'd me thus.*

Alas, he's dead! But can you e'er forget

The tender sorrows and the pangs of nature,

The fond embraces and repeated bleffings,

Which you drew from him in your laft farewel?

Still muft I cherifh the dear, fad remembrance,

At once to torture and to pleafe my foul.

The good old king at parting wrung my hand,

His eyes brim-full of tears, then fighing, cry'd,

Pr'ythee, be careful of my fon. His grief

Swell'd up fo high, he could not utter more.

JUBA.

. Alas, the ftory melts away my foul.

That beft of fathers! How fhall I difcharge

The gratitude and duty, which I owe him?

SYPHAX.

By laying up his counfels in your heart.

---

* *Thefe verfes, from the words,* Sir, your great father, *&c.*
as far as, rather fay your love, *are taken from fcene IV.*
act I.

JUBA.

SYPHAX.

Non me loquentem sic tuus sprevit pater.

Heu vixit! At chara illius an unquam potest

Excidere imago, ubi collo inhærescens tuo,

Mille inter oscula, mille & amplexus, sui

Vix compos, inquit ultimum abituro vale?

Mihi quanto oboritur gaudio immixtus dolor,

Cum dulcè tristem pectore revolvo diem!

Simul ille dextram dexteræ inseruit meæ,

Altúmque ab imo corde suspirans, vide,

Inquit, saluti filii invigiles: simul

Lachrymæ rigabant ora, nec fari dolor

Est plura passus.

JUBA.

Patris ô blandum nimis

Sacrúmque nomen! Fare, quî possim, Syphax,

Præstanda genitori optimo officia exequi.

SYPHAX.

Jussa faciendo.

JUB A.

JUBA.

His counfels bade me yield to thy directions.

SYPHAX.

Alas, my prince, I'd guide you to your fafety.

JUBA.

I do believe, thou wouldft; but tell me how?

SYPHAX.

Fly from the fate, that follows Cæfar's foes.

JUBA.

My father fcorn'd to do it.

SYPHAX.

And therefore dy'd.

JUBA.

Better to die ten thoufand thoufand deaths,
Than wound my honour:

SYPHAX.

JUBA.

Me tuis juſſit pater

Parere monitis.

SYPHAX.

Sola mihi, princeps, tuæ

Cura eſt ſalutis.

JUBA.

Cognitum eſt ſtudium ſatis.

Quid me mones?

SYPHAX.

Quæ Cæſari inimicos premunt,

Ut fata fugias.

JUBA.

Fugere noluit pater.

SYPHAX.

Adeóque periit.

JUBA.

Mille pugnando neces

Subire præſtat, damna quàm famæ pati.

SYPHAX.

SYPHAX.

Rather ſay your love.

JUBA.

. Is it, becauſe the throne of my forefathers
Still ſtands unfill'd, and that Numidia's crown
Hangs doubtful yet, whoſe head it ſhall encloſe,
That thou preſum'ſt to treat thy prince with ſcorn ?

SYPHAX.

Why will you rive my heart with ſuch expreſſions ?*
Does not old Syphax follow you to war ?
What are his aims ? Why does he load with darts
His trembling hand, and cruſh beneath a caſque
His wrinkled brows ? What is it he aſpires to ?
Is it not this ? To ſhed the ſlow remains,
His laſt poor ebb of blood in your defence ?

JUBA.

Syphax, no more ! I would not hear you talk. ·

---

* *Theſe verſes from theſe words,* Is it becauſe, *&c. as far as*
Cæſar I'm wholly thine, *are taken from ſcene V. act II.*

SYPHAX.

Magè dic, amoris.

JUBA.

Fræna verbofæ, Syphax
Injice licentiæ.   An ideò illudere Jubæ
Te poffe credis, quòd patris folium vacat,
Quòd adhuc Numidici nutat imperii decus,
Et me vibrandis imparem fceptris putas ?

SYPHAX.

Cur fic acutis transfodis dictis finum ?
Quid, nonne tecum gradior ad bellum comes,
Fortis fubire & martis & lethi vices ?
Cur lanceâ dextram onero, cur galeâ caput,
Nifi ut reliquias fanguinis, queis hoftica
Manus pepercit, patriæ impendam & tibi ?

JUBA.

Audire plura non libet : Syphax, tace.

SYPHAX.

SYPHAX.

Not hear me talk! What, when my faith to Juba,
My royal mafter's fon, is call'd in queftion?
My prince may ftrike me dead, and I'll be dumb.
But whilft I live, I muft not hold my tongue,
And languifh out old age in his difpleafure.

JUBA.

Thou know'ft the way too well into my heart.
I do believe thee loyal to thy prince.

SYPHAX.

What greater inftance can I give? I've offer'd
To do an action, which my foul abhors,
And gain you, whom you love, at any price.

JUBA.

Was this thy motive? I have been too hafty.

SYPHAX,

SYPHAX.

Jubes Tacere ? Taceat ut Syphax, fides
Cùm data Jubæ in dubium vocatur ? Me Juba
Interimat, & tacebo. Verùm dum traho
Auras fuperftes, luce dum æthereâ fruor,
Nequeo tacere, & principi invifam meo
Ducere feneƈtam.

JUBA.

Corda placandi modum
Artemque nofti. Te mihi fidum reor.

SYPHAX.

Conftare meliùs nempe quî poterat fides ?
Hanc ut probarem, facinus audendi tibi,
Quod abhorret animus, me fore fpopondi ducem ;
Propriam ut haberes Marciam, expedii modum.

JUBA.

An hoc volebas ? Ah nimis præceps fui.

SYPHAX.

SYPHAX.

And 'tis for this, my prince has call'd me traitor.

JUBA.

Sure thou miftak'it.   I did not call thee fo.

SYPHAX.

You did indeed, my prince, you call'd me traitor.

Nay, further, threaten'd you'd complain to *Cato.*

Of what, my prince, would you complain to *Cato?*

That Syphax loves you, and would facrifice ⌐

His life, nay more, his honour in your fervice ?

JUBA.

Syphax, I know thou loveft me.   But indeed,

Thy zeal for Juba carry'd thee too far.

Honour's a facred tie, the law of kings,

The noble mind's diftinguifhing perfection,

That aids, and ftrengthens virtue, where it meets he:

And imitates her actions, where fhe is not.

It ought not to be fported with.

SYPHAX.

SYPHAX.

Ideóque falfum proditorem patriæ
Me nuncupabas.

JUBA.

Num ore quid tale excidit ?
Ancipite peccas fortè deceptus fono.

SYPHAX.

Confilia porrò velle te aiebas mea
Pandere Catoni.   Quæfo, quid tandem Juba
Pandet Catoni ?   Me tibi addictum nimis ?
Me tibi paratum fanguinem & famam quoque
Impendere ?

JUBA.

Tuo te Jubæ addictum fcio.
Sed amore peccafti nimio.   Honefti, Syphax,
Hinc difce leges regibus habendas facras.
Artibus honeftum perpolit mentem fuis,
Virtutis æmulatur abfentis decus,
Præfenti honores afflat imitando novos.

SYPHAX.

SYPHAX.

By heav'ns,

I'm ravifh'd, when you talk thus, tho' you chide me.

Alas, I have hitherto been ufed to think

A blind officious zeal to ferve my king

The ruling principle, that ought to burn,

And quench all others in a fubject's heart.

Happy the people, who preferve their honour

By the fame duties, that oblige their prince !

JUBA.

Syphax, thou now begin'ft to fpeak thyfelf.

Numidia's grown a fcorn among the nations

For breach of public vows.   Our Punic faith

Is infamous, and branded to a proverb.

Syphax, we'll join our cares to purge away

Our country's crimes, and clear her reputation.

SYPHAX.

Believe me, prince, you make old Syphax weep

To hear you talk—but 'tis with tears of joy.

If

SYPHAX.

Per aſtra, penè me mihi rapis, Juba,
Sic quando loqueris.   Id mihi à primâ fuit
Ætate ſuaſum, ſubdito unum hoc eſſe opus,
Unum hunc laborem ; nempe ſe fidum ſuo
Regi approbare.   Beatus is demum fuit,
Qui ſic honeſtum ſimul & officii fidem
Sociare novit.

JUBA.

Syphacis, hîc noſco indolem.
Senſa iſta Syphacem pariter & Jubam decent.
Infamis orbi eſt Punica, ut noſti, fides.
Ne eadem Numidico nomini inſideat nota,
Noſtrum eſt cavere.

SYPHAX.

Ut loqueris, ut places, Juba !
Hâc maĉte, princeps, indole.   I, patrio caput

Diademate

If e'er your father's crown adorn your brows,
Numidia will be blefs'd with *Cato*'s lectures.

JUBA.

Syphax, thy hand! We'll mutually forget
The warmth of youth, and frowardnefs of age.
Thy prince efteems thy worth, and loves thy perfon.
If e'er the fceptre comes into my hand,
Syphax fhall ftand the fecond in my kingdom.

SYPHAX.

Why will you overwhelm my age with kindnefs?
My joy grows burdenfome, I fhan't fupport it.

JUBA.

Syphax, farewel. I'll hence and try to find
Some bleft occafion, that may fet me right
In *Cato*'s thoughts. I'd rather have that man
Approve my deeds, than worlds for my admirers.

[*Exit.*

SYPHAX.

Diademate revinci.   Africæ, I, felix tuæ

Virtutibus Catonis imperium rege.

JUBA.

Amice, dextram junge.   Dictorum damus

Veniam viciffim, mutuam accipimus fidem.

Quando Numidiæ fceptra fumpfero, Syphax

Mihi erit fecundus, proximum regi caput.

SYPHAX.

Nimis ampla amoris pignora accumulas tui.

Vicem referre debitam haud noftræ eft opis.

JUBA.

Syphax, valeto.   Concito hinc greffu feror

Rectâ ad Catonem, fi qua fe fortè offerat

Occafio, viro facta purgandi mea.

Nil curo reliqua, fit modò placidus *Cato*.

[*Exit.*

SYPHAX.

SYPHAX.

Young men foon give and foon forget affronts.

Old age is flow in both.   A falfe old traitor !

Thofe words, rafh boy, may chance to coft thee dear.

My heart had ftill fome foolifh fondnefs for thee.

But hence, 'tis gone.   I give it to the winds.

Cæfar, I'm wholly thine.

SCENE

SYPHAX.

Colligit ut iram leviter, ita leviter premit

Juvenilis ætas: tardus in utroque eſt ſenex.

Ego veterator, proditor, latro ? Hæc tibi

Fortaſſe magno verba conſtiterint, puer.

Amoris antehac nonnihil habebas mei.

Sed hinc faceſſat ; trado rapiendum notis.

Et mente & animo Cæſarem totus ſequor.

I   SCENA

SCENE II.*

SYPHAX, SEMPRONIUS.

SYPHAX.

WELL, *Cato*'s senate is resolv'd to wait
The fury of a siege, before it yields.

SEMPRONIUS.

Syphax, we both were on the verge of fate.
Lucius, declar'd for peace, and terms were offer'd
To *Cato* by a messenger from Cæsar.
Should they submit, e'er our designs are ripe,
We both must perish in the common wreck
Lost in the gen'ral undistinguish'd ruin.

SYPHAX.

But how stands *Cato* ?

* This scene is taken from scene VI. act II.

SEMPRONIUS.

SCENA SECUNDA.

SYPHAX, SEMPRONIUS.

SYPHAX.

FIXUM fenatui ergo, Semproni, fedet
Bello experiri malle fortunam priùs,
Quàm deditâ imperium urbe victoris pati?

SEMPRONIUS.

Quàm penè fati limina attigimus, Syphax?
Auctor ineundæ Lucius pacis fuit,
Pacem Catoni à Cæfare Decius obtulit.
Dii! fi fenatus fœdus accipiat priùs,
Quàm fortiantur noftra confilia exitum,
Actum eft, perivimus.

SYPHAX-

At quid interea *Cato?*

SEMPRONIUS.

SEMPRONIUS.

Thou haſt ſeen mount Atlas.

While ſtorms and tempeſts thunder on its brows,

And oceans break their billows at its feet,

It ſtands unmoved, and glories in its height.

Such is that haughty man. His tow'ring ſoul

'Midſt all the ſhocks and injuries of fortune.

Riſes ſuperior, and looks down on Cæſar.

SYPHAX.

But what's this meſſenger?

SEMPRONIUS.

I've practiſed with him,

And found the means to let the victor know,

That Syphax and Sempronius are his friends.

But let me now examine in my turn.

Is Juba fixt?

SYPHAX.

Yes—but it is to *Cato*.

I've try'd the force of ev'ry reaſon on him,

Sooth'd

SEMPRONIUS.

Vidifti Atlanta. Vertice fuperbo in poli
Minatus aftra inter procellofos notos
Cœlique fulmina arduum attollit caput,
Dum fraĉtus infrà marmore effufo pedem
Tundit furentûm vaftus undarum globus.
Sic ille durus, rigidus, intraĉtabilis
Inter ruinas fortis adverfæ altior
Infurgit, elatóque tumidus Cæfarem
Defpeĉtat oculo.

SYPHAX.

At ille quid porrò Decius ?

SEMPRONIUS.

Illi clam aperui confilî noftri modum ;
Aperiet ille Cæfari. Sed quid mihi
Tu jam viciffim de Jubâ refers,

SYPHAX.

Manet
Fixus Catoni. Cunĉta verfavi, inftiti,

Suafi

Sooth'd and carefs'd, been angry, footh'd again,

Laid fafety, life and int'reft in his fight.

But all are vain; he fcorns them all for *Cato.*

SEMPRONIUS.

Come, 'tis no matter.   We fhall do without him.

He'll make a pretty figure in a triumph,

And ferve to trip before the victor's chariot.

SYPHAX.

But are thy troops prepar'd for a revolt?

Does the fedition catch from man to man,

And run among their ranks?

SEMPRONIUS.

All, all is ready.

The factious leaders are our friends, that fpread

Murmurs and difcontents among the foldiers.

They count their toilfome marches, long fatigues,

Unufual

Suafi, increpavi, voce adulanti preces
Immifcui irâ, rurfus oravi, nihil
Non denique egi, flexus ut tandem puer
Meliora faperet. Perftat immotus tamen
Animis eifdem : opes, falutem & omnia
Uni Catoni devovet.

SEMPRONIUS.

Parvi intereft.

Sic quando libuit, ante victoris rotas
Ductus catenis, nobile triumpho decus,
Alta Capitolia regius fcandat puer.

SYPHAX.

An inter agmina glifcit intereà virûm.
Seditio ?

SEMPRONIUS.

Cæptis exequendis omnia
Parata : voces, murmura, querelæ undique
Palam audiuntur. Factioforum duces
Fremitibus iras militum accendunt fuis,

I 4

Noftrifque

Unufual faftings, and will bear no more
This medley of philofophy and war.

[*A fhout is heard.*

SYPHAX.

What means that fhout, big with the founds of war?*
What new alarm?

SEMPRONIUS.

A fecond louder yet
Swells in the winds, and comes more full upon us.
Within an hour they'll ftorm the fenate-houfe.

SYPHAX.

Make *Cato* fure, and give up Utica.
Mean time I'll draw up my Numidian troops
Within the fquare to exercife their arms,
And as I fee occafion, favour thee.
I laugh to think how your unfhaken *Cato*

---

* *Thefe three verfes, as far as the words,* more full upon me, *are taken from fcene III. act III.*

Will

Noſtriſque ſpondent ſtrenuam inceptis opem.

Parere rigido Stoici imperio ducis

Ultrà recuſant.

[*Clamor tollitur*.

SYPHAX.

Ille quid ſonus refert

Fremens tumultu ? Audin' ut eliſis propè

Clareſcit auris !

SEMPRONIUS.

Curiam hanc ipſam parant

Irrumpere.

SYPHAX.

Catonem arcta conſtringant, vide,

Vincla, & propinqui prodita accipiat jugum

Victoris Utica. Ego interim in foro inſtruam

Turmas equeſtres, promptus, ut fuerit opus,

Succurrere. Hominem quantus invadet ſtupor,

I 5 Cùm

Will look aghaſt, while unforeſeen deſtruction

Pours in upon him thus from every ſide.

[*Exeunt.*

SCENE

Cùm fic ab omni parte glomeratam fciet

In fe rúinam.

[*Exeunt.*

1 6 SCENA

SCENE III.

SEMPRONIUS, with the LEADERS of the MUTINY.

SEMPRONIUS.

AT length the winds are raised, the storm blows high.

Be it your care, my friends, to keep it up

In its full fury, and direct it right,

Till it has spent itself on *Cato*'s head.

Mean while I'll herd among his friends, and seem

One of the number, that whate'er arrive,

My friends, and fellow-soldiers may be safe.

[*Exit.*

FIRST LEADER.

We all are safe. Sempronius is our friend.

Sempronius is as brave a man as *Cato*.

But hark! he enters. Bear up boldly to him.

Be

SCENA TERTIA.

SEMPRONIUS, Conjurati.

SEMPRONIUS.

TURBO jam tandem gravis

Oritur, amici.   Vefter huc tendat labor,

Nec ponat animis detumentibus priùs,

Quàm totus effufo impetu in caput irruat

Catonis.   Ego vultum interea amicum induens

Tanquam fidelis lateri adhærebo comes,

Ut quicquid accidat, integra meorum falus

Commilitonum maneat.

[*Exit.*

CONJ. PRIMUS.

In tuto fumus.

Sempronio aufpice & duce, timendum nihil:

Sempronius par eft Catoni.   Audin, fubit.

Fortiter eundem eft.   Denfi in invifum caput

Geminentur

Be sure you beat him down, and bind him fast.

This day will end our toils, and give us rest.

ALL THE LEADERS.

Fear nothing, Sempronius is our friend.

SCENE

Geminentur ictus, vincula afflictum solo

Ligent ; dies hic ponet ærumnis modum.

OMNES.

Sempronio auspice & duce, timendum nihil.

SCENA

SCENE IV.

CATO, SEMPRONIUS, LUCIUS, PORCIUS, and MARCUS.

CATO.

W HERE are thefe bold intrepid fons of war,
That greatly turn their backs upon the foe,
And to their general fend a brave defiance ?

SEMPRONIUS.

Curfe on their daftard fouls, they ftand aftonifh'd!

[*Afide.*

CATO.

Perfidious men ! And will you thus difhonour
Your paft exploits, and fully all your wars ?
Do you confefs, 'twas not a zeal for Rome,
Nor love of liberty, nor thirft of honour,
Drew you thus far, but hopes to fhare the fpoil
Of conquer'd towns, and plunder'd provinces.

Fir'd

SCENA QUARTA.

CATO, SEMPRONIUS, LUCIUS, PORCIUS,
MARCUS, &c.

CATO.

UBI proditores, acre mavortis genus,
Ignobili adeò terga qui vertunt fugæ,
Et tam virili pectore iacemunt ducem?

SEMPRONIUS.

Styx malè paventes voret! Ut attoniti stupent!

[*Seorſim.*

CATO.

Sic parta bello decora, sic Romam probro
Tanto allinetis, perfidum, ignavum genus?
Num vos honoris ulla, nam quis sit pudor
Verum fateri? num ulla vos laudis sitis,
Amórve libertatis hâc mecum tenus

In

Fir'd with such motives you do well to join

With *Cato*'s foes, and follow Cæfar's banners.

Why did I 'scape th' envenom'd aspic's rage,

And all the fiery monsters of the desert,

To see this day ? Why could not *Cato* fall

Without your guilt ? Behold, ungrateful men,

Behold my bosom naked to your swords,

And let the man, that's injured, strike the blow.

Which of you all suspects, that he is wrong'd,

Or thinks he suffers greater ills than *Cato* ?

Am I distinguish'd from you but by toils,

Superior toils, and heavier weight of cares ?

Painful pre-eminence !

SEMPRONIUS.

By heav'ns they droop !

Confusion to the villains ! All is lost !

[*Aside.*

CATO.

Have you forgotten Lybia's burning waste,

Its barren rocks, parch'd earth, and hills of sand,

Its

In arma traxit ? Nonne vos auri fames,

Provinciarum fpolia, captarum urbium

Convecta præda martis in opus impulit ?

Quin ite, ftudiis hifce flammatos decet

Linquere Catonem & figna Cæfarea fequi.

Cur belluofæ monftra vitavi Africæ ?

Cur tot periclis, cur tot ereptus malis

Ad hoc refervor ? An ut fcelere veftro cadam,

Commilitones ? Licuit at cur non priùs

Scelere alieno cadere ? Sin fixum eft, viri,

Haurite ferro pectora : in vulnus patent.

Et, fi quis à me fe laceffitum putet,

Prior ille feriat.

SEMPRONIUS.

Per Jovem, exanimes tremunt !

Periêre cuncta : vile fucorum genus !

[*Seorfim.*

CATO.

Num tot laborum, quos per immenfos maris

Terræque tractus veftra me feffum falus

Impulit

Its tainted air, and all its broods of poifon?

Who was the firft to try th' untrodden path,

When life was hazarded in ev'ry ftep?

Or, fainting in the long laborious march,

When on the banks of an unlook'd-for ftream

You funk the river with repeated draughts,

Who was the laft in all your hoft, that thirfted?

SEMPRONIUS.

If fome penurious fource by chance appear'd,

Scanty of waters, when you fcoop'd it dry,

And offer'd the full helmet up to *Cato*,

Did he not dafh th' untafted moifture from him?

Did

Impulit adire, pectora oblivio tenet ?

En Lybia, rapidi folis exufta ignibus

Nimiùm propinquis, teftis ante oculos patet ;

Teftes arenæ vafto & inculto folo

Latè jacentes, montium abruptæ minæ,

Putríque paffim omnis venenorum lue

Infecta regio teftis eft recens meis

Calcata plantis. Quis, ubi per loca invia

Cæcófque calles iter erat tentandum, ubi

Greffum inter omnem dubia nutabat falus,

Quis lubricam, inquam, primus invafit viam ?

Aut cùm labore æftúque confecti aridam

Extingueretis amne fortuito fitim,

Crebrífque decrefcentis alvei hauftibus

Raperetis undas, ecquis è tanto virûm

Numero fitivit ultimus ?

SEMPRONIUS.

Si afpera juga

Inter et arenas devio curfu latex,

Siticulofæ

Did he not lead you through the mid-day fun,

And clouds of duft? Did not his temples glow

In the fame fultry winds, and fcorching heats?

CATO.

Hence, worthlefs men! Hence, and complain to Cæfar

You could not undergo the toils of war,

Nor bear the hardfhips, that your leader bore.

LUCIUS.

See, *Cato*, fee th' unhappy men! They weep!

Fear,

Siticulofæ dulce folamen viæ,

Scaturiebat, miles optatos ubi

Certatim in hauftus caderet, atque avidus cavis

Palmífque galeífque ima ficcaret vada,

Patiens ut hic ille Cato dux vefter ftetit,

Plenâque lympham caffide bibendam arido

Rejecit ore! Nonne vobifcum comes

Subter flagrantes folis æftivi faces,

Flatibus eifdem torridi incaluit noti ?

Cur æftuofum pulverem & campum tulit,

Nifi ut labore veftra libertas fuo

Firmata ftaret ? Cedite, ingratum pecus.

CATO.

Ignava bello turba, mavortis probrum,

Ite & querelas Cæfari hinc ferte ociùs,

Laboriofo nempe vos bello impares

Non poffe jam ferre mala, quæ Cato tulit.

LUCIUS.

En ut per ora confcius inerrat pudor !

En

Fear, and remorfe, and forrow for their crime,

Appear in ev'ry look, and plead for mercy.

CATO.

Learn to be honeft men, give up your leaders,

And pardon fhall defcend on all the reft.

SEMPRONIUS.

Cato, commit thefe wretches to my care.

Firft let 'em each be broken on the rack,

Then, with what life remains, impaled and left

To writhe at leifure round the bloody ftake.

There let 'em hang. and taint the fouthern wind.

The partners of their crime will learn obedience,

When they look up and fee their fellow-traitors

Stuck on a fork, and black'ning in the fun.

LUCIUS.

Sempronius, why, why wilt thou urge the fate

Of wretched men ?

SEMPRONIUS.

En lachrymæ, quas fceleris excuffit dolor,
Veniam repofcunt.

CATO.

Colere juftitiam dehinc
Difcite, facinoris prodite rebelles duces,
Ultróque facilem cæteris veniam damus.

SEMPRONIUS.

Plectenda curæ trade mancipia meæ.
Luxata primùm membra rumpantur rotâ,
Sufpenfi ad auftros deinde putrefcant trabe,
Sociis daturi trifte documentum fuis.

LUCIUS.

Cur tam feverus fata miferorum gravas ?

K

SEMPRONIUS.

SEMPRONIUS.

How ! Wouldſt thou clear rebellion ?

Lucius, good man, pities the poor offenders,

That would imbrue their hands in *Cato*'s blood.

CATO.

Forbear, Sempronius ! See they ſuffer death,

But in their deaths remember, they are men.

Strain not the laws to make their tortures grievous.

Lucius, the baſe degen'rate age requires

Severity, and juſtice in its rigour.

This awes an impious, bold, offending world,

Commands obedience, and gives force to laws.

When by juſt vengeance guilty mortals periſh,

The gods behold their puniſhment with pleaſure,

And lay th' up-lifted thunder-bolt aſide.

SEMPRONIUS.

Cato, I execute thy will with pleaſure.

SEMPRONIUS.

Quid? Perduelles crimine abfolvi? Vicem
Sicariorum quippe vir bonus dolet,
Queis tingere manus fanguine Catonis lubet.

CATO.

Sævire nimiùm nec placet, nec nos decet.
Pœna irrogetur.   Dum tamen pœnam irrogas,
Humanitatis efto, Semproni, memor,
Ne fata graviora fubeant, quàm lex finit.
Scelerata, Luci, tempora hæc fummam exigunt
Severitatem.   Hic ille juftitiæ rigor
Reprimit fuperbos, impios terret metu,
Frangit rebelles, legibus vim addit novam.
Vindicta quando debita nocentes premit,
Supplicia fuperi luminibus æquis vident,
Promptáque reductâ fulmina reponunt manu.

SEMPRONIUS.

Imperia lætus exequar.

CATO.

CATO.

Mean-while we'll facrifice to liberty.

Remember, O my friends, the laws, the rights,

The gen'rous plan of power deliver'd down,

From age to age, by your renown'd forefathers,

So dearly bought, the price of fo much blood.

O let it never perifh in your hands,

But pioufly tranfmit it to your children.

Do thou, great Liberty, infpire our fouls,

And make our lives in thy poffeffion happy,

Or our deaths glorious in thy juft defence.

　　　　　　　　　　　　[*Exeunt* Cato, &c.

SCENE

CATO.

Nos interim

Thure precibúfque in vota pofcemus deos.

Queis legibus, quibufve fundatum artibus

Studiífque quondam hoc fuerit imperii decus,

Eftote memores.   Inclytum hunc rerum ordinem,

Tanto labore conditum, ô nunquam, precor,

Sinite perire veftrum in opprobrium, viri.

Verùm quod accepiftis annofo patrum

Tranfmiffum ab ævo pofteris veftris quoque

Tradite fruendum.   Audite, Cœlicolæ, hanc precem.

Adeòque tu nos, magna Libertas, tui

Accende amore ; munere beatos tuo

Exigere liceat liberis vitæ dies,

Vel te tuendo fortiter in acie mori.

[*Exeunt* Cato, *&c.*

SCENA

SCENE V.

SEMPRONIUS, with the LEADERS of the MUTINY.

FIRST LEADER.

SEMPRONIUS, you have acted like yourself.
One would have thought, you had been half in earneft.

SEMPRONIUS.

Villain, ftand off. Bafe, grov'ling, worthlefs wretches,
Mongrels in faction, poor faint-hearted traitors !

SECOND LEADER.

Nay, now you carry it too far, Sempronius.
Throw off the mafk, there are none here but friends.

SEMPRONIUS.

Know, villains, when fuch paltry flaves prefume
To mix in treafon, if the plot fucceeds,
They're thrown neglected by. But if it fails,
They're fure to die like dogs, as you fhall do.

Here,

SCENA QUINTA.

SEMPRONIUS, Conjurati.

CONJ. PRIMUS.

SEMPRONI, es idem femper & fimilis tui.
Te feriò equidem penè credebam loqui.

SEMPRONIUS.

Scelus, hinc faceffe : vile, defpectum caput,
Servile pecus, imbelle fucorum genus !

CONJ. SECUNDUS.

Simulare plura define : haud ultrà his jocis
Eft opus ; amicos, quotquot hîc adftant, vides.

SEMPRONIUS.

Quin fic, fcelefti, accipite ; ubi iftius modi
Mancipia motæ confcias addunt manus
Rebellioni, fi aufa fucceffus habent,
Sine præmio, fine honore neglecti jacent.

Sin

Here, take thefe factious monfters, drag 'em forth
To fudden death.

[*Enter Guards.*

FIRST LEADER.

Nay, fince it comes to this ....

SEMPRONIUS.

Difpatch 'em quick; but firft pluck out their tongues,
Left with their dying breath they fow fedition.

[*Exeunt Guards with the Leaders.*

SCENE

Sin cœpta cedant irrita, nocentes manent

Supplicia certa, miferrimum lethi genus.

Adefto, miles : ad necem hæc monftra ociùs

Abripito.

[*Intrant Satellites.*

CONJ. PRIMUS.

Quando res eò deducitur ....

SEMPRONIUS.

Mandata, liftor, protinus faceffito.

Sed forcipe priùs prendito linguas reis

Atque refecato, ne agmina inter confcia

Novos tumultus voce moribundâ excitent.

[*Exeunt.*

SCENA

SCENE VI.

SYPHAX, SEMPRONIUS.

SYPHAX.

Our firſt deſign, my friend, has prov'd abortive.

SEMPRONIUS.

By *Cato*'s ſtern rebuke diſarm'd at once,
The daſtards ſtood amazed and terrified.

SYPHAX.

Still there remains an after-game to play.
My troops are mounted ; their Numidian ſteeds
Snuff up the wind, and long to ſcour the deſert.
Let but Sempronius head us in our flight,

We'll

SCENA SEXTA.

SYPHAX, SEMPRONIUS.

SYPHAX.

Prima ergo, amice, cœpta cecidêre irrita.

SEMPRONIUS.

Subitâ Catonis voce & afpectu, fui
Oblita turba mente perculfâ ftetit
Attonita, inermis.

SYPHAX.

At novas artes adhuc,
Nova meditor confilia. Frænatis mihi
In equis relucet, quidlibet prompta aggredi
Numidica pubes. Refonat hinnitu procul
Pulfatus æther; ungula impatiens moræ
Impreffa perdit mille veftigia folo,
Corripere dum campum ardet. Age porrò fugæ

K 6

Tu

We'll force the gate, where Marcus keeps his guard,

And hew down all that wou'd oppofe our paffage.

A day will bring us into Cæfar's camp.

SEMPRONIUS.

Thus, Syphax, fhould I fail of half my purpofe.

I'm unreveng'd, if *Cato*'s left behind.

Think not Sempronius can be baffled thus

In his ambition or purfuit of greatnefs.

Syphax, 'tis fixt.   I long to bind in chains

That haughty man, and bear him off to Cæfar.

SYPHAX.

Well faid ! That's fpoken like thyfelf, Sempronius.

SEMPRONIUS.

But how to gain admiffion ? For accefs

Is given to none but Juba and the brothers.

SYPHAX.

Tu ductor efto, quáque ftationes obit
Marcus, ruemus urbe. Pugnando viam
Facilem per obvia quæque fternemus manu.
In Cæfaris caftra feret hodiernus dies.

SEMPRONIUS.

Suadéfne trepidam moliar inultus fugam?
Fallere, Syphax, Sempronium fi fic putas
Abfiftere aufis velle. Vis ingens rapit,
Odium perenne, immenfus irarum dolor.
Cùm perpetrari facinus alienâ nequit,
Manu hâc fuperbum ftringere catenis virum,
Ad Cæfarémque trahere vindicta impotens,
Et mens repulfæ fordidæ impatiens jubet.

SYPHAX.

Virtute tantâ macte. Semproni, inclytum
Meditaris herclè facinus & dignum tui.

SEMPRONIUS.

Ecquâ arte rumpemus aditum? Præter Jubam
Geminófque fratres nemini ingreffus patet.

SYPHAX.

SYPHAX.

Thou shalt have Juba's dress, and Juba's guards.

The doors will open, when Numidia's prince

Seems to appear before the slaves, that watch them.

SEMPRONIUS.

Heav'ns, what a thought is there! The day's our own.

How will my bosom swell with anxious joy,

'When I behold him struggling in his chains,

With shame and grief alternately opprest,

His heart high swol'n, and lab'ring in his breast!

END OF THE THIRD ACT.

ACT

SYPHAX.

Oftro rubenti, quâ folet Juba indui,

Chlamyde indueris ; regiâ incedes caput

Cidari revinctus : Numidicus cinget latus

Satelles. Illicò mancipia pandent fores,

Ubi adeffe regius videbitur puer.

SEMPRONIUS.

Benè eft, beamur. Fata jam vindex manu

Teneo Catonis. Quanta mihi pafcent finum

Gaudia tumentem, ubi turbidus & irâ & probro

Se cernet ille vinculis captum meis

Excutere fruftrà velle victoris jugum !

FINIS ACTUS TERTII.

ACTUS

A C T   IV.

SCENE I.

EMPRONIUS, dreſſed like JUBA, with Numidian Guards.

SEMPRONIUS.

THE deer is lodg'd, I have track'd her to her covert.

Be ſure you mind the word, and when I give it,

Ruſh in at once, and ſeize upon your prey.

Let neither fear, or threats have force to move you.

. . . . . But hark, what noiſe! Death to my hopes!

    'Tis he,

'Tis Juba's ſelf!. There is but one way left.

Hé muſt be murder'd, and a paſſage cut

Thro' thoſe his guards. Hah, daſtards, do you tremble!

Or act like men, or by yon azure heav'n . . . .

SCENE

ACTUS QUARTUS.

SCENA PRIMA.

SEMPRONIUS, vefte Numidica indutus, duo milites.

SEMPRONIUS.

SATELLITES adefte. Difpofitis fera
Laqueis tenetur. Sede quâ lateat, vigil
Oculis notavi. Signa cùm dedero, fimul
Irruite, rapite, avehite prædam. Nec minæ
Nec torvitas fupercilî injiciant metus.
Ingente cœpto digna vos merces manet.
Quid hoc ? Propinquos audio pulfus pedum.
Dii, fallite omen ! Corda fpe dubiâ micant.
Ipfe eft: Juba ipfe gradum admovet. Rerum hoc ftatu
Confulere non eft integrum. Hâc dextrâ cadet:
Rumpenda ferro deinde per medios via.
Audete fortes. Quid, pigro an tremitis metu ?
Animos refumite, vel per aftrorum faces . . . .

SCENA

SCENE II.

JUBA, SEMPRONIUS.

JUBA.

WHAT do I fee? Who's this, that dares ufurp
The guards and habit of Numidia's prince?

SEMPRONIUS.

One, that was born to fcourge thy arrogance,
Prefumptuous youth.

JUBA.

What can this mean? Sempronius!

SEMPRONIUS.

My fword fhall anfwer thee.   Have at thy heart.

JUBA.

Nay, then beware thy one, proud barbarous man.

[*Semp. falls.   His guards furrender.*

SEMPRONIUS.

SCENA SECUNDA.

JUBA, SEMPRONIUS.

JUBA.

QUIS ille tam audax, tam infolens fatellite
Cinctus Numidico infignia ufurpat mea?

SEMPRONIUS.

Vane Afer, animúmque patrio elatum gerens
Faftu, haud ita effugies.

JUBA.

Quid hoc? Sempronius!

SEMPRONIUS.

Hinc fuge, faluti fi effe cònfultum velis.

JUBA.

Quid? me-ne fugere? Afferere famam, cùm tibi
Ita libet infanire, ftat potiùs manu.

[*Educuntur utrinque gladii, pugnatur, cadit Semp.*

SEMPRONIUS.

SEMPRONIUS.

Curfe on my ftars ! Am I then doom'd to fall
By a boy's hand, disfigur'd in a vile
Numidian drefs ? . . . .
Gods, I'm diftracted ! This my clofe of life !
O for a peal of thunder, that would make
Earth, fea, and air, and heav'n, and *Cato* tremble !

                 [*Dies.*

JUBA.

With what a fpring his furious foul broke loofe,
And left the limbs ftill quivering on the ground !
Hence let us carry off thofe flaves to *Cato*,
That we may there at length unravel all
This dark defign, this myftery of fate.

                [*Exeunt.*

                 SCENE

SEMPRONIUS.

Horror Acherontius aftra confundat ftyge.

Sic-ne puerili deftinor victus manu

Effundere animam ? Barbaro-tectus quoque

Humeros amictu ? Struere quis furor impulit

Vincula Catoni ? Rumpite infernas domos

Stygiæ forores, nocteque immerfum infimâ

Caput hoc averno condite æternùm fpecu.

Sic pudet ad umbras ire. Convulfo ruat

Ab axe fulmen, quo penitus æther, mare

Et terra, quo *Cato* ipfe perculfus tremat.

[*Moritur.*

JUBA.

Quanto fub umbras impetu indignans viri

Prorupit animus, membráque etiamnum folo

Liquit trementia ! Miles, hos age fiftito

Servos Catoni, fceleris ut quicquid latet

Dehinc patefcat, confili & caufa & modus.

[*Exeunt.*

SCENA

SCENE III.

PORCIUS, JUBA.

PORCIUS.

SURE 'twas the clash of swords. My troubled heart
Is so cast down, and sunk amidst its sorrows,
It throbs with fear, and akes at every sound.
See, see! here's blood! O see! here's blood and murder!
Hah! a Numidian! Heav'ns preserve the prince!
The face lies muffled up within the garment.
But hah! death to my sight! A diadem,
And purple robes! O gods! 'tis he, 'tis he!
Juba, the loveliest youth, that e'er deserv'd
A Roman's care, Juba lies dead before me!
Stabb'd at his heart, and all besmear'd with blood.*
O he was all made up of charms and virtue,
Whatever maid could wish, or man admire.

* This verse is taken from act III. scene II.

Delight

SCENA TERTIA.

PORCIUS, JUBA.

PORCIUS.

QUIS pepulit aures enfium flictu fonus

Nefcio quis artus turbat infolitus pavor,

Gravibúfque curis anxium pulfat finum.

Quis ille pronus corpore exangui jacet ?

Ah ! Numidam amictus indicat.   Gelidus coit

Sanguis per artus.   Principi timeo.   Latent

Ora involuta vefte.   Proh fuperi ! quid hoc ?

En regia chlamys, regium en frontis decus !

O fcelus ! ô horror ! nullus eft dubio locus.

Eft ipfe Juba.   Juba principum fplendor, decus

Juvenum, voluptas noftra, deliciæ & amor,

Juba indecoro vulnere ante oculos jacet.

Crudelia nimis fata, crudeles deos !

Jacet cruore membra concreto rigens,

Cujus ubi vultus enituit, ibat dies

Gratior,

Delight of ev'ry eye! When he appear'd,

A secret pleasure gladen'd all, that saw him.

But when he talk'd, the proudest Roman blush'd

To hear his virtues, and old age grew wise.

Why do I think on what he was? He's dead!

He's dead, and never knew, how much I lov'd him.

JUBA.

[*Rushing hastily in.*

See, Porcius, see,

The happy Juba lives! He lives to catch

Thy dear embrace, and to return it too.

PORCIUS.

With pleasure and amaze, I stand transported.

Sure 'tis a dream! Dead and alive at once!

If thou art Juba, who lies there?

JUBA.

Gratior, & orbis luce fplendebat novâ.

Heu vana fpes mortalium ! Ut Stygius color

Infecit artus ! Capitis ambrofii decor

Cecidit, nigranti vividum oculorum jubar

Nox texit umbrâ : frigore æterno algida

Silet illa lingua, cujus eloquium Cato

Sæpe ipfe ftupuit. Sed quid ego fruftrà pio

Dolore fluxas repeto virtutes Jubæ ?

Juba Pyladeâ me fide amplexus fuit,

Juba Pyladeâ me fide amplexus perit.

JUBA.

[Derepentè in theatrum erumpens.

Define queri : coram ecce quem defles, adeft.

Et incolumis & vivus en adeft Juba,

Accipere amicum lætus amplexum & dare.

Inter fe complectuntur.

PORCIUS.

Superi ! Quid hoc eft ? Vivis ? An fallax fubit

Imago ? Si vivit Juba, quis ibi jacet ?

JUBA.

A wretch,

Difguis'd like Juba on a curs'd defign.

PORCIUS.

My joy, by beft beloved, and only wifh.

This, this is life, indeed! Life worth preferving.

JUBA.

How fhall I fpeak the tranfport of my foul!

I'm loft in ecftafy! O my dear Porcius!

PORCIUS.

Believe me, prince, before I thought thee dead,

I did not know myfelf, how much I lov'd thee.

JUBA.

O fortunate miftake! O happy Juba!

Fortune, thou now haft made amends for all

Thy paft unkindnefs. I abfolve my ftars.

PORCIUS.

JUBA.

Scelerum magister, regio affumpto Jubam
Mentitus habitu, dum impia oppreffo parat
Vincula Catoni, audaciæ pœnas luit.

PORCIUS.

Benè eft, revixi. O dulce dimidium mei,
Ut voce, ut ore, ut me tuo afpectu beas !

JUBA.

Dilecte Porci, ut tua mihi placet fides !
Vix credidiffem facrum adeò tecum mihi
Interfuiffe vinclum amicitiæ, nifi
Luctûs fuiffem teftis oculatus tui.

PORCIUS.

Neque ipfe nôram, quàm penitus animo, Juba,
Meo infideres, antequam afflixit tuæ
Me mortis error.

JUBA.

Error is felix fuit.
Fortuna ludum ludere levem pertinax
Jam vetera verfâ damna compenfat vice.

PORCIUS.

PORCIUS.

Quick, let us hence. Who knows if Marcus' life

[*Trumpet founds.*

Stand fure ? O Juba, I am warm'd ; my heart

Leaps at the trumpet's voice, and burns for glory.*

[*Exeunt.*

* Almoft all this fcene, changing the names and fome few things, is in fcene III. act IV. The three laft verfes are fpoken by Porcius in fcene III. act III. with this alteration, Marcus' life, inftead of Cato's life.

SCENE

PORCIUS.

Nos hinc ad arma buccinæ clangor vocat.

[*Tuba canit.*

Nimis eſt morarum : fortè jam Marco imminet

Inimicus enſis.   Roma, libertas, ſalus

Nos vocat ad arma.   O ſacra Libertas, manu

Hâc te tueri liceat ! Adverſo æthere

Sin iſta voveo, fortiter in armis mori.

[*Exeunt.*

SCENE IV.

LUCIUS, CATO.

LUCIUS.

I STAND aftonifhed! What, the bold Sempronius,
That ftill broke foremoft thro' the crowd of patriots,
As with a hurricane of zeal tranfported,
And virtuous ev'n to madnefs!

CATO.

Truft me, Lucius,
Our civil difcords have produced fuch crimes,
Such monftrous crimes, I am furpris'd at nothing.
Oh Lucius, I am fick of this bad world!
The day-light and the fun grow painful to me.

ENTER A MESSENGER.*

But fee, where Balbus comes! What means this hafte?
Why are thy looks thus chang'd?

---

* Porcius being a principal perfon in the drama, the tranflator
thought it more becoming the dignity of the ftage to introduce
Balbus as a meffenger, than let Porcius bring and carry meffages.

MESSENGER.

SCENA QUARTA.

LUCIUS, CATO.

LUCIUS.

ATTONITUS hæreo. Quid ? Hoc Sempronius

Hoc acer ille patriæ affertor fuæ ?

Huc omnis ille in Cæfarem effluxit furor ?

CATO.

Haud miror equidem. Sceleris eft adeò nihil,

Quod civium armis noftra non ætas tulit.

O Luci, acerbis animus ægrefcit malis.

Mihi vita gravis eft, lucis æthereæ piget.

INTRAT NUNCIUS.

Quid, Balbe, trepidas ? Summa quo res eft loco ?

BALBUS.

MESSENGER.

My heart is griev'd.
I bring fuch news, as will afflict thee, *Cato.*

CATO.

Has Cæfar fhed more Roman blood ?

MESSENGER.

Not fo.

The traitor Syphax, as within the fquare
He exercifed his troops, the fignal given,
Flew off at once with his Numidian horfe
To the fouth gate, where Marcus holds the watch.
Juba faw, and call'd, but in vain, to ftop him.
He tofs'd his arm aloft, and proudly anfwer'd,
He would not ftay and perifh like Sempronius.

CATO.

BALBUS.

Ne nuncio aures, vereor, afflictas, Cato,
Graviore vulnerem.

CATO.

Eloquere : num plus adhuc
Cæfar Latini fanguinis fudit ?

BALBUS.

Novum
Majúfque, fi quod eft, malum ingruit. Syphax
Veteranus ille prædo, ubi Numidas fuos
Medio ordinârat ludicra exercens foro
Simulacra belli, protinus figno dato,
Cum equitibus abiit transfuga, quà ad auftros patet
Commiffa Marco porta.   Juba fortè obvius
Vidit abeuntem, & nomine inclamans virum
Revocare fruftrà voluit.   Ille altè vibrat
Jactatum in auras brachium, atque atrox refert
Semproniano nolle fc fato mori.

CATO.

Perfidious men ! But Balbus hafte, and fee

That my fon Marcus acts a Roman's part.

[*Exit meffenger.*

Lucius, the torrent bears too hard upon me.

Juftice gives way to force. The conquer'd world

Is Cæfar's. *Cato* has no bufinefs in it.

LUCIUS.

While pride, oppreffion, and injuftice reign,

The world will ftill demand her *Cato*'s prefence.

In pity to mankind, fubmit to Cæfar,

And reconcile thy mighty foul to life.

CATO.

Would Lucius have me live to fwell the number

Of Cæfar's flaves, or by a bafe fubmiffion

Give up the caufe of Rome, and own a tyrant ?

LUCIUS.

The victor never will impofe on *Cato*

Ungen'rous terms. His enemies confefs

The virtues of humanity are Cæfar's.

CATO.

CATO.

Perfida propago ! Sed age tu, Balbe, advola,
Patriæque in armis gloriæ natos mone.

[*Exit nuncius.*

Luci, malorum immenfa me moles premit.
Vi victa cedit juftitia, regnat nefas.
Orbis fubactus Cæfari fervit. Nihil
Opus eft Catone.

LUCIUS.

Quamdiu & fraus & fcelus,
Et amor habendi regnat, erit opus fuo
Orbi Catone. Potiùs, ô potiùs diu
Vive, neque pigeat Cæfaris dono frui.

CATO.

Quid ? Mè-ne vivere patriæ oblitum meæ ?
Vivere tyranni vile mancipium jubes ?

LUCIUS.

Victor Catonem trifte nil coget pati.
Eft comis, eft humana Cæfaris indoles.

CATO.

Curſe on his virtues : they've undone his country.
Such popular humanity is treaſon.

CENE

CATO.

Humana proh viri indoles ! Iſtud nimis

Populare ſtudium patriæ exitio fuit.

SCENA

SCENE V.

CATO, LUCIUS, PORCIUS.

PORCIUS.

MISFORTUNE on misfortune! Grief on grief!
My brother Marcus . . . .

CATO.

Hah, what has he done?
Has he forfook his poft? Has he given way?
Did he look tamely on, and let 'em pafs?

PORCIUS.

Long, at the head of his few faithful friends,
He ftood the fhock of a whole hoft of foes,
'Till obftinately brave, and bent on death,
Oppreft with multitudes he greatly fell.

CATO.

SCENA QUINTA.

CATO, LUCIUS, PORCIUS.

PORCIUS.

INAUSPICATA filii ô fruſtrà pater
Virtute felix, majus ex alio aliud
Malum ingraveſcit, alius exurgit dolor.
Heu Marcus ....

CATO.

Ecquid egit ? An ceſſit loco ?
An fraudulento impunè permiſit duci
Abire ?

PORCIUS.

Cinɛtus fidâ amicorum manu
Totum ingruentis impetum belli tulit,
Par unus omnibus. Animo obnixus diu
Stetit obſtinato, donec excuſſo obrutus
Imbre jaculorum nobili letho occidit.

CATO.

CATO.

I'm fatisfy'd.

PORCIUS.

Nor did he fall before*

His fword had pierc'd thro' the falfe heart of Syphax.

- Yonder he lies.   I faw the hoary traitor

Grin in the pangs of death, and bite the ground.

CATO.

Thanks to the gods! My boy has done his duty.

Porcius, when I am dead, be fure thou place

His urn near mine.

---

* The tranflator, with a view to fet off Porcius's charaćter
with greater luftre, gives him the honour of revenging his brother
Marcus's death by killing Syphax.   This notice will fuffice fur
the reader, who might otherwife be furprifed at the difagreement
between the Verfion and the Original, which it was thought need-
lefs to change.

PORCIUS.

CATO.

Nil plura quæro.

PORCIUS.

Tum mihi animo ardent faces,
'Tum furor & ira perfidum ulcifci fcelus,
Pœnáfque fratre fumere perempto fubit.
Per media præceps agmina Syphacem peto,
Uno in Syphace laboro, fulmineum rotans
Hinc inde ferrum, donec adverfo in finu
Numidæ furentis condidi. Labentem equo
Frendere mediâ in morte confpexi virum,
Et dente pronum mandere cruento folum.

CATO.

Grates tonanti atque reliquis fuperis ago.
Meus eft utérque functus officio puer.
Sibi morte·nomen peperit æternum fuâ
Marcus. Ubi fummam parca fatalem mihi,
Porci, replerit, illius juxta meam,
Vide, locetur urna.

PORCIUS.

PORCIUS.

Long may they keep afunder !

SCENA

PORCIUS.

Ab alterâ altera

Divifa longùm maneat.

SCENE

SCENE VI.

CATO, JUBA, LUCIUS, PORCIUS.

LUCIUS.

BUT fee young Juba! The good youth appears,
Full of the guilt of his perfidious fubjects.

PORCIUS.

Alas, poor prince, his fate deferves compaffion.

JUBA.

I blufh and am confounded to appear
Before thy prefence, *Cato.*

CATO.

What's thy crime?

JUBA.

I'm a Numidian.

CATO.

SCENA SEXTA.

CATO, JUBA, LUCIUS, PORCIUS.

LUCIUS.

E̲N vultum probro

Triſtem à ſuorum ſcelere ſuffuſus ſubit

Juba.

PORCIUS.

Meruit profeƈtò fortunâ frui

Meliore.

JUBA.

Mihi pudor ora, te viſo, *Cato,*

Rubore tingit.

CATO.

Ecquod admiſſum nefas ?

JUBA.

Sum Numida.

CATO.

CATO.

And a brave one too.

Thou haſt a Roman ſoul.

JUBA.

Haſt thou not heard

Of my falſe countrymen ?

CATO.

Alas, young prince,

Falſhood and fraud ſhoot up in ev'ry ſoil,

The product of all climes.   Rome has its Cæſars.

JUBA.

'Tis gen'rous thus to comfort the diſtreſs'd.

CATO.

'Tis juſt to give applauſe, where 'tis deſerv'd.

Thy virtue, prince, has ſtood the teſt of fortune,

Like pureſt gold, that tortur'd in the furnace,

Comes out more bright, and brings forth all its weight.

JUBA.

CATO.

Et illuſtris quoque. Eſt animus tibi
Romanus.

JUBA.

An Syphacis tibi notum ſcelus ?

CATO.

Mala fraus ubique & ſcelera naſcuntur, Juba.
Hæc omnis ætas, omnis hæc regio tulit
Quin ipſa Roma Cæſares habet ſuos.

JUBA.

Eſt indolis generoſæ ita afflicto dare
Solamen.

CATO.

Ubi meretur, eſt æquum dare
Virtuti honorem. Dura te exercet nimis
Fortuna, Juba. Tua clarior virtus tamen
Nitet, & ab ipſis major elucet malis.
Fornace tortum ſic ab ardenti evenit
Auri metallum, decore ſplendeſcens novo.

JUBA.

JUBA.

What fhall I anfwer thee? My ravifh'd heart
O'erflows with fecret joy.   I'd rather gain
Thy praife, O *Cato*, than Numidia's empire.*

LUCIUS.

Now, *Cato*, arm thy foul with all its patience.
See, where the corpfe of thy dead fon approaches!
The citizens and fenators alarm'd
Have gather'd round it, and attend it weeping.

* *The verfes from* But fee young Juba, *&c. as far as*
Numidia's empire, *are taken from fcene IV. act IV.*

SCENE

JUBA.

His quid reponam ? Tacitus exundat finus
Fervétque gaudio.   Tuas malim, *Cato,*
Laudes mereri, quàm Africæ latè potens
Rex imperare.

LUCIUS.

Jam omne premuni, *Cato,*
Virtute pectus.   Mortui en coràm tui
Nati cadaver, trifte fpectaclum fubit.

M   SCENA

SCENE VII.

CATO, JUBA, PORCIUS, LUCIUS, MARCUS'
CORPSE, &c.

CATO.

WELCOME, my son! Here lay him down,
    my friends,

Full in my fight, that I may view at leifure

The bloody corfe, and count thofe glorious wounds.

How beautiful is death, when earn'd by virtue !

Who would not be that youth ? What pity is it,

That we can die but once to ferve our country !

Why fits this fadnefs on your brows, my friends ?

I fhould have blufh'd, if *Cato*'s houfe had ftood

Secure, and flourifh'd in a civil war.

Porcius, behold thy brother, and remember,

Thy life is not thy own, when Rome demands it.

JUBA.

SCENA SEPTIMA.

CATO, JUBA, PORCIUS, LUCIUS, MARCI
CADAVER, &c.

CATO.

SALVETO, nate. . . . . . Hìc onus, amici, poni
Numerare coram vulnera illuſtria juvat,
Corpúſque cernere ſanguine decoro illitum.
Quàm pulchra mors virtute parta, quàm placet!
Ille invidendâ eſt ſorte defunctus puer.
Heu quàm pigendum eſt, quòd ſemel tantùm licet
Impendere animam civium & patriæ bono!
Quis ora, amici, mœſta contriſtat dolor?
Meritò puderet, ſi inter & buſta & faces
Patriæ, Catonis ſtaret incolumis domus.
Porci, ecce fratrem. Illius ab exemplo tuam
Memento vitam, Roma cùm poſcit, tibi
Non eſſe propriam.

JUBA.

JUBA.

Was ever man like this ?

[Aside.

CATO.

Alas, my friends,

Why mourn you thus ? Let not a private lofs

Afflict your hearts.   'Tis Rome requires our tears.

The miftrefs of the world, the feat of empire,

The nurfe of heroes, the delight of gods,

That humbled the proud tyrants of the earth,

And fet the nations free, Rome is no more.

O liberty ! O virtue ! O my country !

JUBA.

Behold that upright man ! Rome fills his eyes

With tears, that flow'd not o'er his own dead fon.

. [Aside.

CATO.

JUBA.

Quem virum unquam orbis tulit
Similem Catoni, heroa quem vidit parem?

[*Seorfim.*

CATO.

Heu, quianam, amici, lachrymis oculi madent?
Privata lachrymis damna deflentur malè,
Quas Roma pofcit. Roma terrarum decus,
Roma dominatrix orbis, imperii caput,
Superûm voluptas, inclyta heroum parens,
Quæ humili tyrannos mundi adæquavit folo,
Gentéfque viɕtrix barbaro exemit jugo,
Heu! Roma fuit. Heu chara libertas fuit!
Heu prifca virtus, patria heu fruftrà meis
Defleta lachrymis!

JUBA.

Magna proh virtus viri!
En Roma lachrymas elicit, quas non fui
Elicere potuit filii exanimis dolor.

[*Seorfim.*

CATO.

CATO.

Whate'er the Roman virtue has fubdued,
The fun's whole courfe, the day and year are Cæfar's.
For him the felf-devoted Decii dy'd,
The Fabii fell, and the great Scipios conquer'd.
Ev'n Pompey fought for Cæfar. Oh my friends!
How is the toil of fate, the work of ages,
The Roman empire fall'n! O curft ambition!
Fall'n into Cæfar's hands! Our great forefathers
Had left him nought to conquer but his country.

JUBA.

While *Cato* lives, Cæfar will blufh to fee
Mankind enflaved, and be afham'd of empire.

CATO.

Cæfar afham'd! Has he not feen Pharfalia!

LUCIUS.

CATO.

Romana quicquid fubdidit virtus, polo

Sub utroque quicquid, quicquid oceanum fupra

Infráque luftrat lucidâ occiduus rotâ

Orienfve Titan, Cæfaris prenfat manus.

Sic Cæfari occidêre Fabii, fic caput

Vovêre Decii, & utérque vicit Scipio.

Imò arma Cæfari ipfe Pompeius tulit.

O dolor, amici ! Ut plurium annorum labor,

Fatorum opus, Romanum ut imperium occidit !

Dominante Cæfare, ô facra ambitio ! occidit.

Quod fubjugaret, nempe majores nihil

Nifi patriam liquêre.

JUBA.

Dum vivit *Cato,*

Mundum erubefcet Cæfar opprimere jugo.

CATO.

Quid ? Ut erubefcat Cæfar ? An non Theffalas

Confpexit acies.

M 4 *LUCIUS.*

LUCIUS.

Cato, 'tis time, thou fave thyfelf and us.

CATO.

Lofe not a thought on me ; I'm out of danger.
Heav'n will not leave me in the victor's hand.
Cæfar fhall never fay, I conquer'd Cato.
But oh ! my friends, your fafety fills my heart
With anxious thoughts. A thoufand fecret terrors
Rife in my foul. How fhall I fave my friends ?
'Tis now, O Cæfar, I begin to fear thee.

LUCIUS.

Cæfar has mercy, if we afk it of him.

CATO.

Then afk it, I conjure you ! Let him know
Whate'er was done againft him, Cato did it.
Add, if you pleafe, that I requeft it of him,

That

LUCIUS.

Hora jam monet *Cato,*

Ut tibi & amicis confulas.

CATO.

Ne vos mei

Cura ulla tangat.   Sum omne difcrimen fupra

Vicéfque fortis.   Cæfar haud unquam inquiet,

Vici Catonem.   Veftra me movet falus.

Vos, vos, amici, reddere incolumes velim !

Hæc fola pectus cura follicitum premit,

Qui vos, amici, reddere incolumes queam.

Cœpi hinc timere Cæfarem.

LUCIUS.

Facilis dabit

Veniam petenti.

CATO.

Petite quin ergo, precor,

Et Cæfar, in fe quicquid eft factum, fciat

Me auctore factum.   Adjicite, fi porrò placet,

Me

That I myſelf, with tears, requeſt it of him,

The virtue of my friends may paſs unpuniſh'd.

Juba, my heart is troubled for thy ſake.

Should I adviſe thee to regain Numidia,

Or ſeek the conqueror?

JUBA.

If I forſake thee,

Whilſt I have life, may heav'n abandon Juba!

CATO.

Thy virtues, prince, if I foreſee aright,

Will one day make thee great.   At Rome hereafter,

'Twill be no crime to have been *Cato*'s friend.

Porcius, draw near! My ſon, thou oft haſt ſeen

Thy ſire engaged in a corrupted ſtate,

Wreſtling with vice and faction.   Now thou ſee'ſt me

Spent, overpower'd, deſpairing of ſucceſs.

Let me adviſe thee to retreat betimes

To thy paternal ſeat, the Sabine field,

Where the great Cenſor toil'd with his own hands,

And

Me supplicis ritu petere, ne quid meos
Peccet in amicos.   Juba, mihi pro te anxius
Laborat animus.   Te-ne victoris sequi
Hortabor arma supplicem, an avitum magis
Repetere regnum Numidiæ ?

JUBA.

Si unquam, *Cato*,
Te deseruero, deserant superi Jubam.

CATO.

Tua ista, princeps, rara virtutum indoles
Tibi decus ingens, nomen & famam afferet.
Ni fallor, illucescet aliquando dies,
Quum justa nullum Roma censebit nefas
Tenuisse cum Catone amicitiam & fidem.
Accede, Porci.   Sæpè vidisti tuum
Cum factione & scelere luctantem patrem :
Nunc spe labanti fessum & exanimem vides.
O nate, ne te pudeat accipere patris
Consilia.   Dum potes, eripe periclis caput,

Et

And all our frugal anceftors were blefs'd
In humble virtues, and a rural life.
There live retir'd, pray for the peace of Rome.
Content thyfelf to be obfcurely good.
When vice prevails, and impious men bear fway,
The poft of honour is a private ftation.

PORCIUS.

I hope, my father does not recommend
A life to Porcius, that he fcorns himfelf.

CATO.

Farewel, my friends! If there be any of you,
Who dare not truft the victor's clemency,
Know there are fhips prepar'd by my command,
Their fails already op'ning to the winds,
That fhall convey you to the wifh'd-for port.
Is there aught elfe, my friends, I can do for you?
The conqueror draws near. Once more farewel!
If e'er we meet hereafter, we fhall meet
In happier climes, and on a fafer fhore,

Where

Et agrum Sabinum, rura majorum, pete,

Ubi magnus olim Cenfor, atque omnes avi

Exigua manibus arva fubigebant fuis,

Virtute mundâ & inope felices lare.

Ibi dulcia inter rura fecretus tuâ

Virtute te involve, patriæ optatam bonus

Pacem precare. Ubi impii imperium obtinent,

Totóque graffatum orbe dominatur fcelus,

Privata meliùs inter obfcuros lares

Sedes honori eft.

PORCIUS.

Num ergo crediderit pater

Me velle vitâ, quam ipfe faftidit, frui ?

CATO.

Valete, amici. Si quibus tutum minùs

Videtur expectare victoris fidem,

Scitote in ipfo ftare jam portu rates

A me paratas. Paffa vela auftros vocant,

In quas velitis cunque deduci plagas.

Quid

Where Cæfar never fhall approach us more.

[*Pointing to bis dead fon.*

'There the brave youth, with love of virtue fired,

Who greatly in his country's caufe expired,

Shall know he conquer'd.   The firm patriot there,,

Who made the welfare of mankind his care,

'Tho'.ftill, by faction, vice, and fortune croft,

Shall find the gen'rous labour was not loft.

END OF THE FOURTH ACT.

ACT

Quid reftat ultrà, quo *Cato* vobis queat

Prodeffe, amici? Victor huc properè advolat.

Iterum valete. Veftra fi pofthac mihi

Videre detur ora, meliori in folo

Feliciore fub axe dabitur, ubi metus

Nullos creabit Cæfar. Ibi fortis puer,

Qui lætus animam patriæ impendit fuæ,

Lauro perenni tempora revinctus fciet

Se fplendidè viciffe. Ibi heroum genus,

Pro civibus amicífque non timidum mori,

Virtute digna præmia accipiet fuâ.

FINIS ACTUS QUARTI.

ACTUS

A C T V.

SCENE I.

CATO Solus.

Sitting in a thoughtful posture. In his hand Plato's book on the Immortality of the Soul. A drawn sword on the table by him.

IT must be so—Plato, thou reason'st well—
Else whence this pleasing hope, this fond desire,
This longing after immortality?
Or whence this secret dread, and inward horror
Of falling into nought? Why shrinks the soul
Back on herself, and startles at destruction?
'Tis the Divinity, that stirs within us.
'Tis heav'n itself, that points out an Hereafter,
And intimates Eternity to man.
Eternity! thou pleasing, dreadful, thought!

Through

ACTUS QUINTUS.

SCENA PRIMA.

C A T O Solus.

Sedet meditanti fimilis, præ manibus habet librum
Platonis de Immortalitate Animæ. In menſâ con-
ſpicitur enſis vaginâ vacuus.

Sic eſſe conſtat. Tu quidem rectè, Plato.

Hæc nempe quorſum blanda ſpes menti inſidet,

Hæc avida deſideria & exardens amor

Æternitatis ? Hic unde ſecretus timor

Horrórque mortis ? Quid animus ſubitô pavet,

Refugítque trepidus, dum olim in antiquum nihil

Metuit relabi ? Numen eſt, quod nos movet.

Divina Mens intus agit. Eſt Deus, Deus,

Totos per artus fuſus, ipſi animo indicans

Æternitatem. Æternitas !—Æternitas !

O dulcis,

Through what variety of untry'd being,

Through what new fcenes and changes muft we pafs ?

The wide, th' unbounded profpeét lies before me ;

But fhadows, clouds, and darknefs, reft upon it.

Here will I hold.   If there's a Pow'r above us,

And that there is all nature cries aloud

Through all her works, He muft delight in virtue ;

And that which he delights in, muft be happy.

But when ? or where ? This world was made for Cæfar.

I'm weary of conjeétures.   This muft end 'em.

> [*Laying his hand on his fword.*

Thus am I doubly arm'd.   My death and life,

My bane and antidote are both before me.

This in a moment brings me to an end ;

But this informs me, I fhall never die.

The

O dulcis !—ò tremenda ! quàm terres—places !

Per quot meatus, quot per ancipites vias

Nováfque formas rerum inexpertum rapis ?

Longè intuenti tractus ille oculis patet

Immenfus, ingens. Atra fed nox incubat,

Spiffæque nubes lumen ambiguum premunt.

Hîc ergo fiftam. Si Deus mundum regit,

At regere pulcher ordo naturæ docet,

Virtute delectatur : & quicquid Deum

Delectat, effe non nequit bonum. Aft ubi,

Quando fruendum ? Totus hic, quantus patet,

Succumbit orbis Cæfari. Dubiis labat

Mens feffa curis. Terminum ponet chalybs.

[Enfi manum admovet.

Mors atque vita fic mihi eft pofita in manu.

Ad utramlibet paratus utramque intuor.

Hic vitam adactâ morte momento rapit,

[Primo enfem,

Mihi fempiternos ille promittit dies.

[deinde librum indicat.

Animus

The foul, fecur'd in her exiftence, fmiles
At the drawn dagger, and defies it point.
The ftars fhall fade away, the fun himfelf
Grow dim with age, and nature fink in years.
But thou fhalt flourifh in immortal youth,
Unhurt amidft the war of elements,
The wrecks of matter, and the crufh of worlds.

What means this heavinefs, that hangs upon me?
This lethargy, that creeps through all my fenfes?
Nature opprefs'd, and harrafs'd out with care,
Sinks down to reft. This once I'll favour her,
That my awaken'd foul may take her flight,
Renew'd in all her ftrength, and frefh with life,
An off'ring fit for heav'n. Let guilt or fear
Difturb man's reft. *Cato* knows neither of 'em,
Indiff'rent in his choice to fleep or die.

SCENE

Animus fuæ immortalitatis confcius

Mucronis aciem ridet & temnit minas.

Tenues vetuftas fiderum extinguet faces,

Ætate fol·ipfe gravis imminuet diem,

Natura tota denique annofam induet

Ultima feneɡam. At animus æternâ nitens

Vivet juventâ. Vivet, & difcors ubi

Elementa bellum fœdere abrupto gerent,

Et fraɡa mundi machina fupremùm gemet,

Illæfus, integer, capite fe alto efferet

Inter ruinas orbiúmque.fragmina.

Sed ecquis artus languor irrepens gravat?

Natura curis laffa fuccumbit fuis,

Requiémque pofcit. Æqua pofcenti obfequar.

Cedam fopori, quò magis animus vigil

Inde renovato robore & vitâ integrâ

Sublime carpat iter ad æthereas domos,

Diis digna fuperis viɡima. Aut timor aut fcelus

Aliis quietem rumpat: ignorat *Cato*

Utrumque, mortem placidus an fomnum eligat.

SCENA

SCENE II.

C A T O, P O R C I U S.

CATO.

BUT hah! how's this, my son? Why this intrusion
Were not my orders, that I would be private?
Why am I disobey'd?

PORCIUS.

Alas, my father,
What means this sword, this instrument of death?
Let me convey it hence!

CATO.

Rash youth, forbear.

PORCIUS.

O let the pray'rs, th' intreaties of your friends,
Their tears, their common danger wrest it from you.

CATO:

SCENA SECUNDA.

CATO, PORCIUS.

CATO.

PORCI, quid hoc? Quorfum hæc, vel unde audacia?

Non imperâram, ne quis huc ferret pedem?

Cur nate, cur fic juffa violantur mea?

PORCIUS.

Dilecte genitor, ifte quid gladius minax,

Strictus, neci paratus? O precor, fine,

Sine hinc removeam!

CATO.

Define imprudens puer.

PORCIUS.

Tibi hunc tuorum lachrymæ, & vota & preces,

Communéque periclum omnium è manibus, pater,

Extorqueant, oro.

CATO.

CATO.

Would'ft thou betray me ? Would'ft thou give me up
A flave, a captive, into Cæfar's hands ?
Retire, and learn obedience to a father,
Or know, young man ! ....

PORCIUS.

      Look not thus fternly on me.
You know, I'd rather die, than difobey you.

CATO.

'Tis well ! Again I'm mafter of myfelf.
Now, Cæfar, let thy troops befet our gates,
And bar each avenue, thy gath'ring fleets
O'erfpread the fea, and ftop up ev'ry port :
Cato fhall open to himfelf a paffage,
And mock thy hopes.

PORCIUS.

CATO.

Quid ? An hofti prodere ?
An fervituti, an Cæfari, an vinclis dare
Me vis inermum ? Hinc illicò faceffe, & patri
Obtemperare difce, vel nôris, puer ...

PORCIUS.

Ah quid ita me torvùm afpicis ? Vultum, precor,
Exue minacem. Levius eft mortem pati,
Quam patris iram. Nulla me cernet dies
Inobfequentem.

CATO.

Sanguinem agnofco meum.
Jam denuò eft mihi liberum arbitrium meæ
Vitæ necis-ve. Cinge jam, Cæfar, viris
Hanc undique urbem, milite frequenti exitus
Portúfque claude, & claffibus totum tuis
Infterne pontum, liberam *Cato* viam
Sibi ipfe aperiet, fpéfque deludet tuas.

PORCIUS.

PORCIUS.

O Sir, forgive your fon,

Whofe grief hangs heavy on him ? O my father!

How am I fure it is not the laft time

I e'er fhall call you fo ? Be not difpleafed,

O be not angry with me, whilft I weep,

And, in the anguifh of my heart, befeech you

To quit the dreadful purpofe of your foul!

CATO.

Thou haft been ever good and dutiful.

[*Embracing him.*

Weep not, my fon ; all will be well again.

The righteous gods, whom I have fought to pleafe,

Will fuccour *Cato*, and preferve his children.

PORCIUS.

Your words give comfort to my drooping heart.

CATO.

Porcius, thou may'ft rely upon my conduct.

Thy father will not act what mifbecomes him.

But

PORCIUS.

O parce nato, genitor. Incumbens dolor
Gravis intus anxium finum opprimit. . O pater,
Te nunc fupremùm forfan appello patrem,
His parce lachrymis, neve fuccenfe ; & locus
Si quis datur adhuc precibus, hanc mentem exue.

CATO.

Bonus fuifti femper & patri obfequens.
Abfterge lachrymas : cunſta reftituet dies.
Quos demerere, nate, mihi femper meâ
Pietate ftudui, Dii patrem & natos tegent.

PORCIUS.

Mihi pectus ægrum dicta folantur tua.

CATO.

Porci, timores mitte : fe indignum *Cato* .
Nil perpetrabit. Vade jam nate, & vide,
Nihil ut amicis defit : afcendant rates.

Si

But go, my fon, and fee if aught be wanting

Among thy father's friends.   See them embark'd;

And tell me if the winds and feas befriend them.

My foul is quite weigh'd down with care, and afks

The foft refrefhment of a moment's fleep.

[*Exit.*

SCENE

Si placida maria dent foluturis noti,

Mihi deinde refer.   Exhaufta mens curis labat,

Brevífque fomni lene folamen petit.

[*Exit.*

SCENA

SCENE III.

P O R C I U S, . J U B A.

PORCIUS.

MY thoughts are more at eafe, my heart revives.
I feel a dawn of hope break in upon me.
My father will not caft away a life,
So needful to us all, and to his country.

ENTER JUBA.

JUBA.

Where is your father, Porcius, where is *Cato ?*

PORCIUS.

Juba, fpeak low, he is retired to reft.

SCENA TERTIA.

PORCIUS, JUBA.

PORCIUS.

ANIMO parumper pulfus eſt triſti dolor,
Spéſque orta rebus melior afflictis venit.
Auguria niſi vana capio, haud unquam manu
Suâ ipſe vitæ tempora abrumpet pater,
Cujus adeò opus habet orbis, & Roma, et ſui.

INTRAT JUBA.

JUBA.

Tuus ubi, Porci, genitor? Ubi *Cato?*

PORCIUS.

Cave,

Submiſſa leni verba referantur ſono.
Somnum reclinis lectulo invitat levem.

JUBA.

JUBA.

Alas, I tremble when I think on *Cato*,
In every view, in every thought I tremble!
Cato is stern, and awful as a God.

PORCIUS.

Though stern and awful to the foes of Rome,
He is all goodnefs, Juba, always mild,
Compaffionate and gentle to his friends,
Fill'd with domeftic tendernefs, the beft,
The kindefs father. I have ever found him
Eafy, and good, and bounteous to my wifhes.

JUBA.

JUBA.

Horrore quodam mens mihi facro tremit,
Quoties Catonem cogito. Tanquam Deus
Aliquis ab alto lapfus, auguftus, gravis,
Rigidus, feverus, & tremendus eft *Cato.*

PORCIUS.

Gravis & tremendus hoftibus Romæ licèt,
Eft bonus amicis, placidus & mitis fuis.
Primis ab annis Porcio talis fuit,
Amans, benignus, facilis, indulgens pater.

JUBA.

Neque Porcio uni : pariter eft femper finu
Jubam paterno, ut fanguinem amplexus fuum.
Hinc & viciffim ego filii officio ut patrem
Et amore colui, magna virtutum fequi
Veftigia avidus.

PORCIUS.

Inde par decus enitet
Jubæ & Catonis.

N 5

JUBA.

JUBA.

'Tis his confent alone can make me blefs'd.

Could I but call that wond'rous man my father,*

I might be blefs'd.   But who knows *Cato*'s thoughts?

PORCIUS.

He is retired to reft, and feems to cherifh

Thoughts full of peace.   He has difpatch'd me hence

With orders, that befpeak a mind compofed,

And ftudious for the fafety of his friends.

Juba, take care that none difturb his flumbers.

---

* Taken from act I. fcene II. and fpoken by Sempronius in the original.

SCENE

JUBA.

Ille me folus poteft
Facere beatum.   Fas mihi ô utinam foret
Socerum vocare ! At ecqua turbato gerat
Confilia tacitus pectore, incertum latet.

PORCIUS.

Confilia pacis mollia videtur fui
Securus agere.   Sola amicorum falus
Facit inquietum.   Hinc ire me ad portum jubet,
Ubi paffa ventos carbafa morantes vocant.
Ne quis reclinem turbet, interea vide.

SCENA

SCENE IV.

J U B A Solus.

O YE immortal Powers, that guard the juſt,
Watch round his couch and ſoften his repoſe.
Baniſh his ſorrows, and becalm his ſoul
With eaſy dreams : remember all his virtues,
And ſhew mankind, that goodneſs is your care.

SCENE

SCENA QUARTA.

JUBA Solus.

Dii fofpitales, quotquot humanum genus

Terráfque regitis, fi qua refpeÄant pios

Numina, Catonem cernite. Vigili torum

Cingite coronâ, & pellite infomnes metus.

Placido fopore viÄus abfiftat dolor,

Levibúfque mentem fomniis pafcat quies

Dulcis & amica. Meruit hoc virtus viri.

Hinc quotquot orbem vaftum & immenfum incolunt,

Studiáque virtutéfque juftorum fciant

Diis effe curæ.

SCENA

SCENE V.

LUCIUS, JUBA.

LUCIUS.

SWEET are the flumbers of the virtuous man.

O Juba, I have feen the godlike *Cato*.

Some power invifible fupports his foul,

And bears it up in all its wonted greatnefs.

A kind refrefhing fleep is fall'n upon him,

I faw him ftretch'd at eafe, his fancy loft

In pleafing dreams.   As I drew near his couch,

He fmiled, and cry'd, Cæfar, thou can'ft not hurt me.

JUBA.

SCENA QUINTA.

LUCIUS, JUBA.

LUCIUS.

MEMBRA divinus *Cato*
Leni fopore laxat. Ipfe alto toro
Vidi jacentem, proh virum qualem, Juba!
Diis vix minorem. Priftino innixum fuæ
Vigore mentis tela fortunæ fupra
Aliquis potenti fublevat manu Deus.
Toro fupinum blanda dum mulcet quies,
Tranquillus animo varia, quæ finxit fopor,
Simulacra rerum deviam mentem abftrahunt,
Placidifque ludunt fomniis. Tacito pede
Propiùs ut acceffi, ore fubridens, levi
Voce inquiebat; jam mihi, Cæfar, nequis
Nocere: tutus arma tua temnit *Cato.*

JUBA.

JUBA.

His mind ftill labours with fome dreadful thought.
My blood runs cold*; my frighted thoughts fly back,
And ftartle into madnefs . . . .

LUCIUS.

Away! you're too fufpicious. All is fafe†,
While *Cato* lives. His prefence will protect us.
Cæfar is ftill difpofed, to give us terms,
And waits at diftance, till he hears from *Cato*.

* Taken from act III. fcene II. † Ibid. fcene III.

JUBA.

JUBA.

Nefcio, quid animo turbidus cæco parat

Ingens, tremendum. Gelidus in venis cruor

Formidine coit, horror invadit finum.

Deliberata fortè mors tutum facit.

LUCIUS.

Nimios timores pone : qui vigilem folet,

Vel fomniantem fuftinet animi vigor.

JUBA.

Novi Catonem. Vincula indocilis pati,

Nunquam probrofo colla fubmittet jugo.

Jam quoque propinquus hoftis infeftis metum

Adauget armis.

LUCIUS.

Dum fuis *Cato* intereft,

Metus omnis abfit. Ipfe nos teget, hoftibus

Vel nunc tremendus. Pronus ad veniam, moras

Innectit ultrò Cæfar, ut tandem *Cato*

Remittat animum, oblatam & accipiat fidem.

JUBA.

JUBA.

No, no; the horfemen are return'd from viewing
The number, ftrength, and pofture of our foes,
Who now encamp within a fhort hour's march.
On the high point of yon bright weftern tower
We ken them from afar, the fetting fun
Plays on their fhining arms and burning helmets,
And covers all the field with gleams of fire.

LUCIUS.

Juba, 'tis time we fhould awaken *Cato*.

JUBA.

Vana ominaris. Miſſus hoſtiles eques
Luſtrare numeros nunciat in urbem redux
Propè imminere Cæſarem. Ipſa ad mœnia
Brevis hora ſiſtet. Turre ab excelſâ, obvios
Quæ ſpeĉtat auſtros, agmine inſtruĉto licet
Proſpicere turmas. Sol ut oceanum ſubit
Adverſa in arma lucidos ignes vibrat ;
Galeæque clypeíque ære rutilanti vomunt
Ferale fulgur, arváque accendunt novis
Radiata flammis.

LUCIUS.

Illicò è ſomnis *Cato*
Eſt excitandus. Commodùm à portu redux
En Porcius adeſt.

SCENA

SCENE VI.

JUBA, PORCIUS, LUCIUS.

JUBA.

PORCIUS, thy looks fpeak fomething of impor-
  tance.
What tidings doft thou bring? Methinks I fee
Unufual gladnefs fparkling in thy eyes.

PORCIUS.

As I was hafting to the port, where now
My father's friends, impatient for a paffage,
Accufe the ling'ring winds, a fail arrived
From Pompey's fon, who, through the realms of Spain
Calls out for vengeance on his father's death,
And roufes the whole nation up to arms.
Were *Cato* at their head, once more might Rome
Affert her rights, and claim her liberty.

                                    But

SCENA SEXTA.

JUBA, PORCIUS, LUCIUS.

JUBA.

F ARE quid, Porci, refers.

Infolita in oculis figna lætitiæ micant.

PORCIUS.

Modò ut petebam concito portum gradu,

Miffus ab Iberâ lembus advenit plagâ,

Pompeius ubi junior, magni patris

Juratus ultor, bella molitur nova,

Totáfque ad arma in Cæfarem gentes ciet.

His fe ducem præbere fi vellet *Cato,*

Populus Quirini denuò poffet fua

Afferere jura, & lapfa libertas polo

Revifere

But hark ! · What means that groan ?

            [*A groan is heard.*

LUCIUS.

Cato, amidſt his ſlumbers thinks on Rome,
And in the wild diſorder of his ſoul

          ´   [*Another groan.*

Mourns o'er his country.   Hah ! a ſecond groan ...
Heav'n guard us all.

            [*Exit Lucius.*

PORCIUS.

      Alas, 'tis not the voice
Of one who ſleeps ! 'Tis agonizing pain,
'Tis death is in that ſound. O ! ſhould my father ...
I die away with horror at the thought.*

       * Act IV. ſcene III.

                        JUBA.

Revifere orbem numine erectum fuo.

[*Auditur gemitus.*

Ah! ecquid audio? unde lamentabilis

Venit ifte gemitus?

LUCIUS.

Somno ut indulget *Cato*,

Alto repoftam cogitat Romam finu ;

Dúmque vagus animum turbidum fopor rapit,

Lugubre fatum patriæ & cafum ingemit.

[*Alter gemitus.*

Ah rurfus ingemit! Malum, ô fuperi, precor,

Avertite omen.

Exit Lucius.

PORCIUS.

Somnus haud tales folet

Ciere gemitus.   Morte vox gravis fonat :

Eſt ille fupremus animam efflantis labor.

Ah, Juba, timeo! Mihi corda lethalis pavor

Micantia haurit.   Nefcio, quod ingens malum

Præfagit animus.

JUBA.

JUBA.

O Porcius, hope and fear rife up at once,†

And with variety of pain diftract me.

RE-ENTER LUCIUS.

LUCIUS.

O fight of woe ! . . . .

What we fear'd, O Porcius, is come to pafs !

Cato is fall'n upon his fword.   I've raifed him up,

And placed him in his chair, where pale and faint

He gafps for breath.

JUBA.

No more, no more, O Lucius !

Hide all the horrors of thy mournful tale,

And let us guefs the reft.

PORCIUS.

O Juba, Juba,

Have I not caufe to rave and beat my breaft,

To rend my heart with grief, and run diftracted ? ‡

---

† Act III. fcene I.   ‡ Act IV. fcene III.

JUBA.

JUBA.

Non minor me cura habet,
Dum ſpes metúſque hinc inde dubitantem rapit.

L U C I U S REDIT.

LUCIUS.

Crudele fatum ! Verus heu nimiùm timor !
Mori obſtinatus incubuit enſi *Cato*.
Suo volutum ſanguine erexi ſolo.
Cathedrâ repoſtus, pallidus, languens trahit
Ægros anhelitus.   Sinu ingens plaga hiaſ.

JUBA.

O parce, Luci, parce lachrymabili
Aures ferire nuncio.   Mente liceat
Conjicere reliqua.

PORCIUS.

Luctus ô quantus meo
Incumbit animo.

O   *JUBA.*

JUBA.

Now, Porcius, now call up to thy affiftance
Thy wonted ftrength and conftancy of mind :
Thou can'ft not put it to a greater trial.

PORCIUS.

O Juba, I'm diftrefs'd, I ftand aftonifh'd *
Like one juft blafted by a ftroke from heav'n,
Who pants for breath, and ftiffens, yet alive
In dreadful looks, a monument of wrath !
    Now tell me, Juba, tell me from thy foul,†
If thou believeft, 'tis poffible for man
To fuffer greater ills, than Porcius fuffers ?

JUBA.

O Porcius, Porcius ! might my big fwoll'n heart
Vent all its griefs and give a loofe to forrow,
Juba could anfwer thee in fighs, keep pace
With all thy woes, and count out tear for tear.

------

* Aȼt III. fcene II.   † Aȼt IV. fcene I.

PORCIUS.

JUBA.

- Prome nunc omnem tui

Conſtantiam animi, & pectus obfirma malis.

PORCIUS.

Totus-perhorreſco, velut inopino Jovis

Qui tactus igni palpitat, anhelat, pavet,

Vitæque penè neſcius vivit ſuæ.

Siccine mihi, pater optime, ereptus peris?

Siccine pericula inter & belli minas

Deſeris amicos? O mî Oreſtæâ fide

Primis ab annis cognite, ô animo meo

Chariſſime Juba, fare, num' tandem putas

Majora poſſe perpeti quenquam mala,

Quàm Porcius perpetitur?

JUBA.

O Porci, meum

Si cor dolori liberum frænum daret,

Juba tibi, Porci, paribus afflictus malis

Lachrymam rependet lachrymâ, gemitum pari

Gemitu rependet.

O 2   PORCIUS.

PORCIUS.

Hence let me fly into my father's prefence, *
And pay the laft fad duties.

LUCIUS.

His weeping fervants,
Obfequious to his orders, bear him hither.
Full of compaffion, as his life flows from him,
He inftantly demands to fee his friends. †

* Act V. fcene IV.   † Act V. fcene IV.

SCENE

PORCIUS.

Sinite, in obſequia patris,
Ultima, priuſquam ſpiritum exhalet, ruam.

LUCIUS.

Vernæ obſequentes huc ferunt. Senſim fugit
Dum vita labris, ultimùm affari ſuos
Natum atque amicos voce moribundâ rogat.

SCENA

SCENE VII.

CATO brought in a chair, JUBA, PORCIUS,
LUCIUS, Senators, &c.

PORCIUS.

O HEAV'N, affift me in this dreadful hour !

LUCIUS.

Now is Rome fall'n indeed !

JUBA.

Thefe are thy triumphs,
Thy exploits, O Cæfar !

CATO.

Here fet me down.
Porcius, come near me.　Are my friends embark'd ?
Can any thing be thought of for their fervice ?

Whilft

SCENA SEPTIMA.

CATO cathedrâ fubvectus, JUBA, PORCIUS, LUCIUS, Senatores, &c.

PORCIUS.

DII, luctuofâ Porcio hâc horâ, precor,
Succurrite, & benè ferre fortunam date.

LUCIUS.

Jam Roma ab alto culmine everfa occidit.

JUBA.

En, en facinora, ô Cæfar, eñ laurus tuæ,
Tui en triumphi!

CATO.

Me, viri, hîc deponite.
Accede, Porci. Vela num ventis mei
Dedêre amici? Num quid eft adhuc fupcr,
Suos juvare quo ampliùs poffit *Cato*.

O 4　　　　　　　　Dum

Whilſt I yet live, let me not live in vain.

O Lucius, art thou here ? Thou art too good.

Let this our friendſhip live between our children.

Make Porcius happy in thy daughter Lucia.

Alas, poor man, he weeps ! Marcia, my daughter,

O bend me forward ! Juba loves thee, Marcia.

A ſenator of Rome, while Rome ſurvived,

Would not have match'd his daughter with a king.

But Cæſar's arms have thrown down all diſtinction.

Whoe'er is brave and virtuous, is a Roman.

I'm ſick to death.   O when ſhall I get looſe

From this vain world, th' abode of guilt and ſorrow !

And yet methinks a beam of light breaks in

On my departing ſoul.   Alas, I fear

I've been too haſty.   O ye Pow'rs, that ſearch

The heart of man, and weigh his inmoſt thoughts,

If

Dum vivo, ne fruſtrà, precor, vivam. Ut caret

Anteaꞓa labe vita, liceat ad ultimum

Dixiſſe, Vixi. Te-ne, mi Luci, intuor ?

Eſt grata pietas. Quæ mihi tecum fuit,

Uſque ſacra noſtris vivat in natis fides,

Juba—ô relapſum paululum inclina—Juba,

Pietas tua eſt mihi nota, notus eſt amor.

Dum ſalva ſtabat Roma, Romanus foret

Senator indignatus externum ſibi

E regiâ ſtirpe generum. At rerum omnia

Diſcrimina enſe ſuſtulit Cæſar ſuo.

Quicunque pulchrâ laude virtutis nitet,

Romanus audit.—Ægra mors triſti caput

Involvit umbrâ.—O quando corporeo anima

Carcere ſoluta ſordidam effugiet humum,

Sedem hanc malorum & ſceleris odioſam domum ?

Tamen ſupremum dum fugax iter parat,

Videtur illi lucis æthereæ jubar

Illabi ab alto.—Ah ! vereor, ut præceps nimis

Facinus patrârit dextera ! O Superi, O deûm

O 5   Hominúmque

If I have done amifs, impute it not !

The beft may err, but you are good, and oh !

[*Dies.*

LUCIUS.

There fled the greateft foul, that ever warm'd
A Roman breaft.   O *Cato !* O my friend !
Thy will fhall be religioufly obferv'd.

JUBA.

But let us bear this awful corpfe to Cæfar,
And lay it in his fight, that it may ftand
A fence betwixt us and the victor's wrath.
Cato, tho' dead, fhall ftill protect his friends.

LUCIUS.

Hominúmque rector, cuncta qui justò æstimas

Momenta rerum, & mentis humanæ intimos

Lustras receffus, si quid erravi, precor,

Ne verte crimini. Hominis est crrare. At, oh !

Moritur.

LUCIUS.

En civis ille funere indigno perit,

Quo justiorem Roma non unquam parens

Sinu educavit. O mihi fruftrà *Cato*

Dilecte, terris quando te polus invidet,

Habebo femper hunc honoratum diem,

Semper & acerbum.

JUBA.

Funebri pompâ interim

Corpus feramus Cæfari. Motu licèt

Et luce caffus proteget amicos *Cato.*

Ubi Catonis cernet exuvias fuo

Sanguine decoras victor; oblitus feræ

Manfuefcet iræ.

LUCIUS.

LUCIUS.

From hence, let fierce contending nations know,

What dire effects from civil difcords flow.

'Tis this, that fhakes our country with alarms,

And gives up Rome a prey to Roman arms ;

Produces fraud, and cruelty, and ftrife,

And robs the guilty world of *Cato*'s life.

[*Exeunt omnes.*

LUCIUS.

Hinc concitæ gentes gravi

Difcant duello, quanta procudit mala

Difcòrdium armis civium accenfus furor.

Concuffa ab alto vertice hinc patria ruit,

Telífque Roma fraĉta Romanis jacet.

Hinc fraus & omnis criminum emerfit cohors,

Raptufque nobis vixit heu ! fruftrà *Cato.*

[*Exeunt omnes.*

ALEXANDER's FEAST;

OR THE

POWER of MUSIC.

AN

ODE on St. CECILIA's DAY.

By Mr. DRYDEN.

DONE INTO LATIN VERSE.

ALEXANDER's FEAST.

AN ODE.

'TWAS at the royal feaft, for Perfia won

By Philip's warlike fon,

    Aloft in awful ftate .

    The god-like hero fat

On his imperial throne.

    The lovely Thais by his fide

    Sat like a blooming eaftern bride,

    `In flow'r of youth and beauty's pride.

  Happy, happy, happy pair,

    None but the brave,

    None but the brave

None but the brave deferves the fair.

                   His

ALEXANDRI CONVIVIUM.

CARMEN.

———————

REGIFICO quondam, devictâ Perfide, luxu
Cùm ftrueret menfas proles generofa Philippi,
Ipfe, genus divûm, folio fublimis ab alto
Sefe compofuit cænæ, mediumque locavit.
Suavè rubens Thais, Tithoni conjugis inftar,
Affedit lateri, viridi formofa juventâ.
Felices ambo : tanto quippe illa marito
Digna fuit, tali dignus fuit hic quoque fponfâ,

Belligeri

His valiant peers were placed around,

Their brows with roſes and with myrtle bound.

So ſhould deſert in arms be crown'd.

  Timotheus placed on high

   Amid the tuneful quire,

    With flying fingers touch'd the lyre:

   The trembling notes aſcend the ſky,

    And heav'nly joys inſpire.

   The ſong began from Jove,

   Who left his bliſsful ſeats above.

   A dragon's fiery form belied the God;

   Sublime on radiant ſpheres he rode,

   When he to fair Olympia preſs'd

   To court the beauties of her ſnowy breaſt.

  . . . .

  . . . .

        The

Belligeri proceres, focii comitefque laborum,

Myrtis atque rofis redimiti tempora circùm

Læti adfunt, ftratoque fuper difcumbitur oftro.

Tantus honos armis, tantæ eft victoria laudis.

Timotheus confeffum inter turbamque canentûm

Tractat agens citharam, digitifque micantibus omnes

Explorans numeros, vario modulamine chordas

Protinus impellit, rapidoque repercutit ictu.

Lætitiâ plaufuque fremunt, ftudiifque calentes

Exultant convivæ, animofque ad fidera tollunt.

A Jove principium : Jovis omnia plena canebat.

Ille fupercilio celfi moderator olympi

Cuncta movet, cælorum orbes pontumque profundum.

Ille corufcanti nimborum in nocte, tonanti

Turbine

The lift'ning crowd admire the lofty found.

A prefent Deity they fhout around,

A prefent Deity the vaulted roofs rebound.

    With ravifh'd ears

    The monarch hears,

      Affumes the god,

      Affects to nod,

    And feems to fhake the fpheres.

The praife of Bacchus then the fweet mufician fung,

Of Bacchus ever fair and ever young.

    The jolly god in triumph comes,

    Sound the trumpets, beat the drums,

      Flufh'd with a purple grace

      He fhows his honeft face.

    Now give the hautboys breath, he comes, he come

      Bacchus ever fair and young,

      Drinking joys did firft ordain.

                                      Bacchus'

Turbine contorquet fulmen, quo percita tellus,

Quo mortale genus trepidant et numen adorant.*

Talibus arreêtæ mentes agitataque corda

Grajugenûm.   Deus, ecce deus vox omnibus una,

Et deus, ecce deus laquearia pulfa reclamant.

Attonitus rex ipfe audit : fimul enthea mentem

Vis fublimè rapit, mediifque interferit aftris.

Jamque nihil mortale petens fuper æthera viêtor

Fertur ovans, nutuque quatit deus alter olympum.

Plurimus in Bacchi laudes formamque decoram

Deinde canit vates inconfumptamque juventam.

Evoe lætitiæ Bacchus dator advenit, alto

Edomitas Nifæ fleêtens de vertice tigrès.

Argutos adeò fundat cava tibia cantus,

Majori clangore fonent lituique tubæque,

Et fremebunda ftrepant repetito tympana pulfu.

Purpureum oftentans fuffufo lumine vultum

Bacchus adeft, rofeufque aulam fubit hofpes apertàm.

Bacchus honoratas leges fervare bibendi

---

* The reader will here undoubtedly notice, and, we truft,
approve a fhort deviation from the loofe original.

Bacchus' bleffings are a treafure,

Drinking is the foldier's pleafure.

Rich the treafure,

Sweet the pleafure,

Sweet is pleafure after pain.

Sooth'd with the found, the king grew vain,

Fought all his battles o'er again,

And thrice he routed all his foes, and thrice he flew

the flain.

The mafter faw the madnefs rife,

His glowing cheeks, his ardent eyes,

And while he heav'n and earth defied,

Changed his hand, and check'd his pride.

He chofe a mournful mufe

Soft pity to infufe.

He fung Darius great and good,

By too fevere a fate

Fall'n, fall'n, fall'n, fall'n, fall'n from his high eftate

And welt'ring in his blood.

Deferted

Inftituit primus, concordes inter amicos
Inftaurare dapes, et pocula ponere menfis.
Quis poft vina gravem martem durofque labores
Conqueritur ? Poft martis opus durofque labores
Infanire juvat, dulcemque haurire furorem.

Talia dum memorat, faftu turgefcere inani
Rex acer, fævoque iterum contendere bello.
Ter ftravit ftratos, et fufa ter agmina fudit.·
Jam tumido trepidare finu, torvoque tueri
Lumine, jam martem vultu fignare cruento.
Dumque ardens adeò terris minitatur et aftris,
Atque ipfos demens vocat in certamina divos,
Flebilis in querulam, converfo pectine, mufam
Barbiton inflectit vates; ea fræna furenti
Subjicit, et ftimulos fub pectore vertit amaros.
Darium illuftrem, quo non pacatior alter
Extiterat terris, regali à culmine lapfum,
Afflictumque folo, proh triftia fata, canebat.·

Verniles

Deferted at his utmoft need

By thofe his former bounty fed,

On the bare earth expofed he lies,

With not a friend to clofe his eyes.

With down-caft look the joylefs victor fat,

Revolving in his alter'd foul

The various turns of fate below,

And now and then a figh he ftole,

And tears began to flow.

The mighty mafter fmiled to fee,

That love was in the next degree.

'Twas but a kindred found to move,

For pity melts the mind to love.

Softly fweet in Lydian meafures

Soon he footh'd his foul to pleafures.

War, he fung, is toil and trouble,

Honour but an empty bubble.

Never

Verniles animæ, proceres jam in morte relinquunt

Exanguem, nec adeft, qui languida lumina claudat.

Trifte fedet victor, mutatâ mente revolvens

Fataque, fortunafque virûm, variofque labores.

Mox gemitus mæfto de corde dat interruptos

Sufpirans, lachrymifque humectat grandibus ora.

Ipfe fibi plaudit vates; jamque acer eodem

Pectine, quo ftravit, geftit relevare jacentem. .

Lydorum doctus numeros dulcemque Camænam,

Leniùs attrectat citharam, placidoque canore

Senfim abolet curas, blandumque infpirat amorem.

Inftructas nequicquam acies, iterataque magnis

Prælia commemorat cœptis, Mavortis acuti

Sanguineos ludos, vacuos et honore triumphos.

P   O quem

Never ending, ftill beginning,

Fighting ftill, and ftill deftroying;

If the world be worth thy winning,

Think, O think it worth enjoying.

Lovely Thais fits befide thee,

Take the good the gods provide thee.

The many rend the fkies with loud applaufe;

So love was crown'd, but Mufic won the caufe.

The prince, unable to conceal his pain,

Gazed on the fair,

Who caufed his care;

And figh'd and look'd,

Sigh'd and look'd,-

Sigh'd and look'd, and figh'd again.

At length with love and wine at once opprefs'd,

The vanquifh'd victor funk upon her breaft.

Now ftrike the golden lyre again,

And louder yet, and yet a louder ftrain.

Break his bands of fleep afunder,

And roufe him up like a rattling peal of thunder.

O quem facra fames, et inexfaturabilis ardor

Per tot inexhauftos cafus triftefque ruinas

Abripit armorum, quem per tot bella ruentem

Gloriæ adhuc urget, laudifque infana cupido,

Quam tandem ftatues metam, rex magne, laborum?

Si fuerat tanti victoria digna laboris,

Eft propriâ mercede labor quoque dignus, et ipfos

Victores fua dona manent.   Age, carpe diei

Gaudia, quæque tenes, præfentibus utere donis.

Sic regi placitum : linguis plaufuque faventûm

Atria longa fonant : ferit aurea fidera clamor.

Talia laurigero virtus ornata triumpho

Præmia habet, victrix retulit fed mufica palmam.

Junctus Amor Baccho mediâ jam regnat in aula,

Cui vix attollens nutantia lumina princeps

Pugnat adhuc, tumido poffit fi pectore Divum

Excutere, infufo donec jam numine victus,

Succumbit fomno pariter vinoque gravatus.

Hark, hark, the horrid found

Has raifed up his head,

As awaked from the dead,

And amazed he ftares around.

Revenge, revenge, Timotheus cries,

See the furies arife,

See the fnakes, that they rear,

How they hifs in their hair,

And the fparkles, that flafh from their eyes !

See a ghaftly band,

Each a torch in his hand !

Thefe are Grecian ghofts, that in battle were flain,

And unburied remain,

Inglorious on the plain.

Give the vegeance due

To the valiant crew.

Behold, how they tofs their torches on high,

How they point to the Perfian abodes

And glitt'ring temples of their hoftile gods !

'The

Nunc age, nunc citharam rurfus convelle fonantem,

Acriter increpitans : nunc ceu ruat axe tonanti

Terrificum fulmen, rauco cava buccina cantu

Cornuaque et litui, geminataque tympana rumpant

Vincla fopora viro.   Tali dum murmure circùm

Cuncta ftrepunt, nigris velut experrectus ab umbris,

Rex levat attonitus caput, et perftricta repenti

Corda pavore tremens vaga lumina circumflectit.

Jam mora nulla tenet, pœnas vindicta repofcit,

'Timotheus clamat : viden, ut de nocte profundâ

Difcurrunt furiæ ! Viden, ut fub crinibus angues

Scintillant oculos, horrendaque fibila tollunt !

En tædis armata cohors, en agmina bello

Adverfo proftrata graves de Perfide pœnas

Solicitant.   Hæc omnis inops inhumataque turba

Graiorum eft : pœnas cuncti fimul ore repofcunt.

Surge adeò et vindex ulcifcere fata tuorum.

Afpicis, ut rutilos intentant hoftibus ignes,

Attolluntque faces irati, et templa deorum

Perfarum exitio fignant devota futuro.

The princes applaud with a furious joy,

And the king feized a flambeau with zeal to deftroy.

　　　　Thais led the way

　　　　To light him to his prey,

And like another Helen fired another Troy.

　　　　Thus long ago,

Ere heaving bellows learn'd to blow,

While organs yet were mute,

Timotheus to his breathing flute

And founding lyre,

Could fwell the foul to rage, or kindle foft defire.

　　　At laft divine Cecilia came,

　　　Inventrefs of the vocal frame.

The fweet enthufiaft from her facred ftore

　　　Enlarged the former narrow bounds,

　　　And added length to folemn founds,

With nature's mother wit and arts unknown before.

　　　Let old Timotheus yield the prize,

　　　　Or both divide the crown,

　　　He raifed a mortal to the fkies,

　　　　She drew an angel down.

Protinus arreptam spirans immanè corufcat

Rex pinûm, pofcitque amens incendia victor.

Confpirant plaufu proceres, cunctique fequuntur.

Ipfa inter medios, tædâ flagrante, tumultus

Prima micat Thais, cæci dux fæmina facti,

Alteram et incendit ceu Tyndaris altera Trojam.

Sic citharâ quondam fretus fidibufque, priufquam

Organa adhuc norant animata tumefcere flatu,

Timotheus varios acuit fub pectore motus,

Indomitamque iram, placidûmque accendit amorem.

Cæcilis at tandem patriis defcendit ab aftris

Docta modos fuperûm.   Divino numine plena,

Illa novos juffit numeros clarefcere terris,

Ignotoque priùs grandefcere carmina cantu.

Timotheus adeò palmam concedat ovanti

Cæciliæ, aut meritam capiant fimul ambo coronam.

Ille potens numeris mortalem ad fidera vexit,

Hæc cæli indigenam deduxit ab æthere divum.

ODE for MUSIC,

on

S. CECILIA's DAY.

By Mr. POPE.

DESCEND, ye nine, descend and sing;
The breathing instruments inspire,
Wake into voice each silent string,
And sweep the sounding lyre !
　　In a sadly-pleasing strain
　　Let the warbling lute complain ;
　　　Let the loud trumpet sound,
　　　'Till the roofs all around,
　　　The shrill echoes rebound :

　　　　　　　　　　　While

IN LAUDEM MUSICES

IN

DIE S. CÆCILIÆ SACRO.

CARMEN.

 AONIIS defcende jugis, age funde canoros,
Turba novena; modos : fpiranti carmina buxo
Suffice, & in numeros citharam moderata tacentem,
Protinus impulfo quate fila fonantia plectro.

Flebilis in molles longùm vibrata querelas
Dulcè gemat teftudo, ftrepant lituique tubæque,
Et pulfata volet circum laquearia clangor.
Pleniùs interea lento folemnia flatu

P 5   Organa

While in more lengthen'd notes and flow,
The deep, majeſtic, ſolemn organs blow.

Hark ! the numbers ſoft and clear,
Gently ſteal upon the ear ;
Now louder, and yet louder riſe,
And fill with ſpreading ſounds the ſkies ;
Exulting, in triumph, now ſwell the bold notes,
In broken air, trembling, the wild muſic floats ;
'Till, by degrees, remote and ſmall,
The ſtrains decay,
And melt away,
In a dying, dying fall.

By muſic minds an equal temper know,
Nor ſwell too high, nor ſink too low.
If in the breaſt tumultuous joys ariſe,
Muſic her ſoft, aſſuaſive voice applies :
Or when the ſoul is preſs'd with cares,
Exalts her in enlivening airs.

Warriors

Organa clarefcant, exultantique canore

Ventofis reddant modulatam follibus auram.

Audin ! lene melos blandè fubrepit in aures.

Jam magis atque magis latè fe fundit, & ipfis

Acceptum fuperis emittit ad aftra fonorem.

Et tumet, & tremit, & plaudit, geminatque, trium-
   phatque,

Elifumque modis trepidantibus aëra complet.

Mox cæfim extenuat fefe, numerofque minutim

Expirat moriens, & deficit expirando.

Dirigit arte fuâ moderatrix mufica mentem,

Nec torpere finit nimiùmve tumefcere ; pectus

Gaudia fi mixto turbent exorta tumultu,

Illa regit numeris motus, & pectora placat.

Sin animus jaceat curarum pondere preffus,

Ipfa fubit, curafque levat, recreatque jacentem.

Warriors fhe-fires with animated founds;

Pours balm into the bleeding lover's wounds.

  Melancholy lifts her head,

  Morpheus rouzes from his bed,

  Sloth unfolds her arms and wakes,

  Lift'ning Envy drops her fnakes:

Inteftine war no more our Paffions wage,

And giddy Factions bear away their rage.

But when our country's caufe provokes to arms,

How martial mufic ev'ry bofom warms!

So when the firft bold veffel dared the feas,

High on the ftern the Thracian raifed his ftrain,

  While Argo faw her kindred trees

  Defcend from Pelion to the main.

        Tranfported

Bellatorum animis virtutem accendit, & ægro

Sufficit occultè medicans lenimen amanti.

Ipfius ad numeros curas jubet ire folutas

Mœftitia ; è ftratis excitus corripit artus

Morpheus ; Pigrities torpentes excutit ulnas,

Protinus evigilans ; fopitis anguibus adftat

Invidia, & modulos avidâ bibit aure fonoros.

Inteftina filent animorum bella ; quiefcit

Seditio, pofitas nec jam reminifcitur iras.

At cùm bella vocant, armorumque ingruit horror,

Martius ut lituûm fonitus clangorque tubarum

Exacuit mentem, patriæque accendit amore !

Sic ubi prima ratis, curfus tentare minaces

Audax, ignotis pelagi fe credidit undis,

Threïcius vates puppi fublimis ab altâ

Increpuit citharam ; cognatas, nec mora, pinus

Peliacis vidit defcendere montibus Argo.

Lætitiâ

Tranſported demi-gods ſtood round,

And men grew heroes at the ſound,

Enflam'd with glory's charms :

Each chief his ſev'nfold ſhield diſplay'd

And half unſheath'd the ſhining blade ;

And ſeas, and rocks, and ſkies rebound

To arms, to arms, to arms.

But when thro' all th' infernal bounds,

Which fláming Phlegethon ſurrounds,

Sad Orpheus ſought his conſort loſt,

Th' inexorable gates were barr'd ;

And nought was ſeen, and nought was heard,

Around the dreary coaſt,

But dreadful gleams,

Diſmal ſcreams,

Fires that glow,

Shrieks of woe,

Sullen moans,

Hollow groins,

And cries of tortur'd ghoſts.

Lætitiâ circùm, plaufuque animifque frementes,

Semidei exultant reges, martemque laceffunt.

Ufque·adeò pulchræ flagrantia corda fatigat

Laudis amor. Clypei textos feptemplicis orbes

Heros quifque rotat ; vaginæ damnat inertes

Exiliens jam mucro moras : vox omnibus arma,

Rupes arma, fretumque polufque arma, arma remittunt.

Sed raptam Eurydicem cùm per lachrymabile Ditis

Inferni regnum, rápidus flagrantibus undis

Quod Phlegeton ambit, gemebundus quæreretOrpheus,

Objice crudeles non exorabile limen

Præclufêre fores. Hîc caligantia circum

Littora terrificæ voces, lamenta, gravefque

Mifceri gemitus, & lugubres ululatus.

Continuò nigræ torrenti vortice peftes

Flammarum erumpunt, & latè lurida jactant

Fulgura ; tum ftridor ferri, tortoque flagello

Verbera, & umbrarum planctus refonare nocentûm.

Fallor !

But hark ! he ſtrikes the golden lyre ;

And ſee ! the tortur'd ghoſts reſpire.

 See, ſhady forms advance !

Thy ſtone, O Siſyphus, ſtands ſtill ;

Ixion reſts upon his wheel,

 And the pale ſpectres dance.

The Furies ſink upon their iron beds

And ſnakes uncurl'd hang liſt'ning round their heads.

 By the ſtreams that ever flow,

 By the fragrant winds that blow

  O'er th' Elyſian flow'rs ;

 By thoſe happy ſouls, who dwell

 In yellow meads of Aſphodel,

  Or Amaranthine bow'rs :

 By the heroes armed ſhades,

Glitt'ring thro' the gloomy glades,

       By

Fallor ! Threïcio crepuit chelys aurea plectro ?

Lætæ respirant pœnis cessantibus umbræ.

Exangues plaudunt choreas ad carmina Manes :

Turba levis propiore movet vestigia passu.

Non jam Ixionei circùm rota vertitur orbis,

Nec saxum Æoliden revolubile Sisyphon urget.

Oblitæ irarum, Furiæ se in strata reclinant

Ferrea, & intenti pendent de crinibus angues.

Per Stygis æternò labentia flumina, dixit,

Per Zephyrum, qui lenè volans per amœna vireta

Elysios flores fragranti recreat aurâ ;

Per fortunatas animas, manesque piorum,

Asphodelo qui prata tenent flaventia, vel quos

Frondibus intextis redolens Amaranthus inumbrat ;

Perque heroum umbras, ferroque auroque micantes,

Quæ tremulam vibrant nemora inter nubila lucem ;

Per

By the youths that died for love,

Wand'ring in the myrtle grove,

Reſtore, reſtore Eurydice to life:

Oh take the huſband, or return the wife.

He ſung, and hell conſented

To hear the Poet's pray'r:

Stern Proſerpine relented;

And gave him back the fair.

Thus ſong could prevail

O'er death, and o'er hell,

A conqueſt how hard, and how glorious?

Tho' fate had faſt bound her

With Styx nine times round her,

Yet muſic and love were victorious.

But ſoon, too ſoon, the lover turns his eyes:

Again ſhe falls, again ſhe dies, ſhe dies!

How wilt thou now the fatal fiſters move?

No crime was thine, if 'tis no crime to love.

Now

Per, quos fævus amor crudeli tabe peredit,

Secretique tegunt calles & myrtea fylva ;

O precor, Eurydices properata retexite fata ;

O date, mecum iterum fupera ut convexa revifat !

Id fi Parca vetat,——letho gaudete duorum.

Talibus orabat : nigri facraria Ditis,

Haud mora, confeafêre ; ratafque Proferpina juffit

Effe preces. Quid non adeò Lethoque Ereboque

Mufica devictis fperet fuperare canende ?

Obftabant fera fata licèt, reditumque nigranti

Claudebat novies Styx circumfufa palude,

Vicit amor, citharâ pollens fidibufque canoris.

Aft incautus amans nimiùm citò refpicit : illa

Heu ! retro ad Stygias collapfa revolvitur umbras.

Quâ prece, quo fletu Manes jam flexeris, Orpheu ?

Crimen abeft, ni fortè nimis fit crimen amâffe.

Nunc

Now under hanging mountains,

Beſide the falls of fountains,

Or where Hebrus wanders,

Rolling in Mæanders,

    All alone,

    Unheard, unknown,

    He makes his moan,

    And calls her ghoſt,

For ever, ever, ever loſt !

Now with Furies ſurrounded,

Deſpairing, confounded,

He trembles, he glows,

Amidſt Rhodope's ſnows.

See, wild as the winds, o'er the deſert he flies ;

Hark ! Hæmus reſounds with the Bacchanals cries—

    Ah ſee, he dies !

Yet ev'n in death Eurydice he ſung,

Eurydice ſtill trembled on his tongue,

    Eurydice the woods,

    Eurydice the floods,

Eurydice the rocks, and hollow mountains rung.

Nunc quà defeſſus variis erroribus undas

Hebrus agit, five abrupti ſub fragmine montis

Surda ſedens inter pronarum murmura aquarum,

Nulli exauditus, lachrymans, ignotus, acerbùm

Ingemit, & queſtu montes ſylvaſque fatigat,

Eurydicem ingeminans & non revocabile fatum.

Nunc ſtupet attonitus, furiis agitatus, & expes;

Dum Rhodopen luſtrat glacie nivibuſque regentem,

Ardet, & ardentem tremor occupat.   Ilicet amens

Per loca vaſta fugit properantibus ocyor Euris.

Thyrſigeris audin' bacchantibus inſonat Hæmus—

Heu! miſer occidit!—At miſeram tamen algida lingua,

Ah miſeram Eurydicem, vitâ fugiente, ciebat.

Eurydicen ſylvæ, Eurydicen amneſque lacuſque,

Eurydicen montes, & concava ſaxa ſonabant.

Muſa

Muſic the fierceſt griefs can charm,

And fate's ſevereſt rage diſarm :

Muſic can ſoften pain to eaſe,

And make deſpair and madneſs pleaſe :

Our joys below it can improve,

And antedate the bliſs above.

This the divine Cecilia found,

And to her Maker's praiſe confin'd the ſound.

When the full organ joins the tuneful quire,

Th' immortal pow'rs incline their ear ;

Borne on the ſwelling notes our ſouls aſpire,

While ſolemn airs improve the ſacred fire,

And Angels lean from heav'n to hear.

Of Orpheus now no more let Poets tell,

To bright Cecilia greater pow'r is giv'n ;

His numbers raiſed a ſhade from hell,

Hers lift the ſoul to heav'n.

Mufa regit luctufque feros, legemque feveram
Fatorum : infufâ duram dulcedine mutat
Pœnarum rabiem, & blando folamine mulcet
Lymphatos animos defperantefque falutis.
Lætitiæ majore replet mortalia fenfu
Pectora, datque alti præfcifcere gaudia cœli.

Hoc, afflata Dei propiori numine, fenfit
Cæcilis, & modulos cœlo facravit & aris.
Cùm conjuncta choris pleno modulamine plaudunt
Organa, concentum cupidis gens incola cœli
Auribus accipiunt.   Sacro fimul igne calentes,
Nos quoque in æthereos animis fublimibus orbes
Abripimur, cœlumque ipfum penetramus ovantes.

Threïcium ceffent adeò jam dicere vates
Orphea ; Cæciliæ major conceffa poteftas.
Conjugis hic manes Stygiis revocavit ab umbris,
Illa canens fublimè levat fuper æthera mentem.

Quatuor

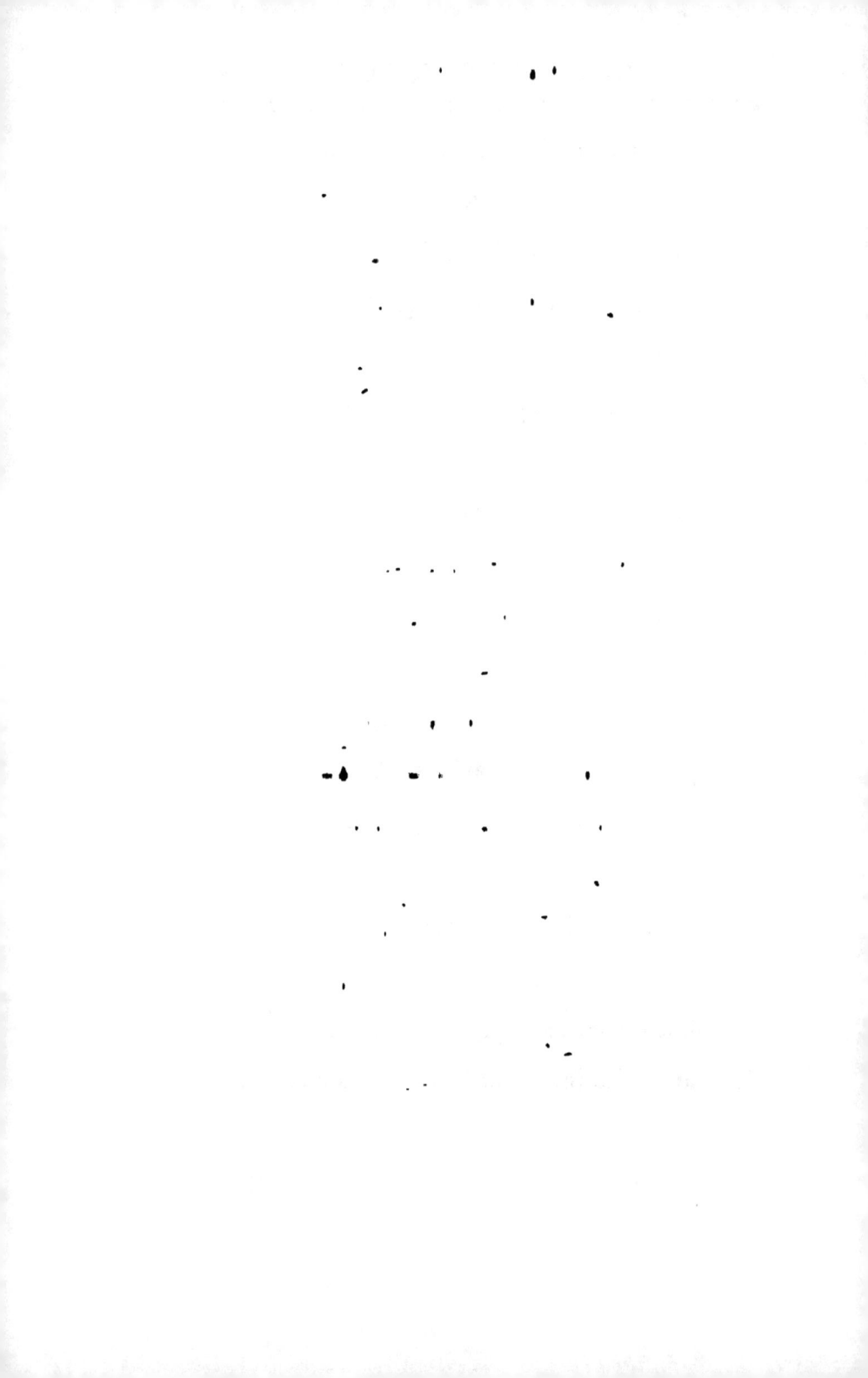

Quatuor vertentis anni Tempeſtates.*

CARMEN.

AREA lata jacet multo nitidiſſima culta

Herbarum florumque toris, quam quatuor albo

Marmore Nympharum vivos referentia vultus

Diſtinguunt ſimulachra, loci ornamenta ſuperbi.

Hinc via porrigitur raris interſita lucis,

Quantùm acie poſſunt oculi luſtrare tuentûm.

Ordine directo ſurgunt æqualibus inter

Se ſpatiis ulmi, cælo capita alta ferentes.

Parte ex adverſâ, nigrâ nemus imminet umbrâ,

Luxurie foliorum horrens : hîc aurea mala,

* Anglicè The Seaſons. Vide Spectator, Vol. 6, N. 425.

Q   Laurique

Laurique et falices et amantes littora myrti.

Amnis utrumque latus vitreâ pellucidus undâ

Alluit, et terram viridanti gramine veftit.

Tractus amore loci greffum huc, ut fæpe, ferebam.

Jam pronus Titan immerferat æquore currum,

Et vefpertinos accenderat Hefperus ignes.

Cynthia jam puro furgens effulget olympo,

Et tremulos philomela modos merulæque canoræ

Certatim exorfæ replent concentibus auras.

Unda repercuffæ radians ab imagine lunæ,

Et lenes zephyrorum animæ, mollefque fufurri

Infolitâ mentem recreant dulcedine, et omnes

Curas ire jubent. O terque quaterque beati,

Queis fani, aiebam, tanta inter gaudia ruris

Contigit innocuæ traducere tempora vitæ !

His ego deliciis pigram excuffiffe feneétam

Optârim, lapfæque annos renovare juventæ.

Tum vario expendi labentia tempora motu,

Volventifque anni tempeftatumque per orbem

Continuos reditus : ut nox vaga fidera promit,

Et

Et peritura diem nafcentem aurora reducit:

Quid facit infeftas hyemes, quo fidere findit

Sol æftivus agros, primo quot vere colores

Florea terra parit, quantas autumnus opimo

Fundit opes gremio, donec jam bruma recurrens

Excutit arboribus, quos ver renovârat honores.

Talia volventi placuit pendente fub ulmo

Sternere corpus humi: nec longùm ita fortè jacenti,

Incertum florúmne aurâ ftudióve diurno,

Paulatim obrepens fufos fopor occupat artus.

In fomnis ecce ante oculos placidiffimus horti

Vifus adeffe mihi Genius, quem ponè fequuntur

Horæque et Menfes, anni vertentis imago.

Emicat ante alios viridi fpectabilis ævo,

Egregius formâ Juvenis.* Decor æmulus aftris

Fronte fedet; crines divinum vertice odorem

---

* Ver.

Exhalant

Exhalant, veſtiſque pedes deſcendit ad imos
Serica, textorum vernans ſubtemine florum.
Ætas prima licèt nondum ſortita virile
Robur erat, florente tamen juſtâque figurâ
Membrorum incedit, qualem decet eſſe juventæ.
Dextram ornat croceo narciſſus junétus acantho,
Purpureiſque roſæ circumdant tempora ſertis.
Hujus in adventu ſeſe natura fragrantes
Induit in flores.   Molli de ceſpite ſurgunt
Sub pedibus violæ, panditque decora tenellum
Primula per campos folium, primæva Favonî
Et Chloris ſoboles.   Novus hinc Vertumnus amiétu
Verſicolore nitet, viridrs incinéta capillos
Flora roſis illinc greſſum comitatur euntis.

Hæc perluſtranti mihi dum miranda videntur,
Ecce repercuſſos lunæ ſplendentis ab orbe
Flamma, illapſa oculis, radios ad nubila jaétat.
Talibus attonitus viſis, huc protinus ambas
Fleéto acies, habitumque viri greſſumque tremiſco.

Per

Per campum incedit rutulis circumdatus armis
Pugnator, strictoque nemus praefulgurat enfe.
Pectus et ampli humeri nitidâ pro vefte teguntur
Loricâ confertâ hamis : frontem premit ærea caffis.
Fare, ifthæc quæ forma viri, vifûque tremendum
Os bellatoris ? Quæ tanta licentia ferri ?
Cui Genius : quem tu, trepidus formidine, campo
Profpicis adverfo gradientem et torva tuentem,
Bellipotens Mars eft, qui quanquam fanguine gaudet,
Non tamen ufque furit ; clypeique oblitus et haftæ,
Interdum properat vernis fe jungere Nymphis.

Nunc placito juxtà Charitum chorus agmine prodit,
Implicitis pariter manibus zonifque folutis,
Ad citharæ cantum per prata virentia feftas
Exercent choreas : ventis dant colla comafque,
Alternifque folum pulfant ex ordine plantis.
Innumeris ftipata Jocis Venus aurea lucet
In medio, blandoque omnes fupereminet ore.
Inclufum vitro folem Titaniaque aftra

Circumfert

Circumfert lævâ, fceptrum regale corufcat

Dextrâ, fceptrum auro gemmifque micantibus aptum.

Inde retrò verni fuccedunt ordine Menfes.

Martium ut adverfum vidi per amæna vireta

Ferre pedem, vifus primùm mihi vultus et ora

Nubibus obduci, et fulcari tempora rugis.

Aft ubi jam cæpit propiore accedere paffu,

Turbida paulatim nigræ rarefcere frontis

Nubila, et æthereas fefe purgare fub auras.

Jam facies tam blanda nitet, jam tanta relucet

Gratia, jam rifu tam temperat ora fereno,

Ut cognofcendi ftudio juvet ufque morari,

Et conferre gradum, mentemque explere tuendo.

Ordo fed intereà rapitur revolubilis anni,

Nec fine triftitiæ fenfu difcedere vidi,

Florigero quamvis aditum patefecit Aprili.

Ille ubi jam propiùs per amica filentia lunæ

Acceffit, formam egregiam vultumque falubrem

Luftravi

Luſtravi admirans: adeò illi dulcis inerrat

Temperies, leni tantus color inſidet ore !

Quà graditur, vernum ſequitur decus: omnis in herbam

Turgida ſurgit humus, zephyriſque tepentibus halant

Purpurei flores. Terris tamen aurea condit

Lumina nonnunquam, et dubiæ caligine frontis

Squalentem glomerans nubem ſe ſolvit in imbres

Irriguos: primam rurſus mox colligit ore

Temperiem, nubeſque fugat ſolemque reducit.

Illius admiſſo Maius veſtigia curſu,

Urget anhelanti ſimilis. Conṭenta parato

Tela tenens arcu gradientem paſſibus æquat

Natus Acidaliæ Veneris: jam jamque ſagittam

Emiſſurus erat, quando ut tranſibat, amantûm

Continuò auditi fletus, lamenta, querelæque,

Et fraſtæ gemitu voces. Sed leniter aures

Vix feriunt, ubi jam ſtridenti turbine venti

Omnia confundunt et nubibus irrita donant.

Talia

Talia miranti, magnâ comitante catervâ,

Apparet nova forma Viri ;* graditurque per hortum

Jam medium, et profugi veſtigia veris anhelo

Paſſu urget, viridefque umbras fontefque requirit

Impatiens æſtûs.   Humeris projecerat altis

Cirratas errare comas et ludere vento.

Olli roriferas fupra caput explicat alas

Crinibus alludens Zephyrus, folifque calentes

Defendit radios, et flamine mulcet amico.

Huic bini comites ſtipant latus ; Hefperus albo

Veſtus equo, et croceis rutilans Aurora capillis.

Pan et flava Ceres, manibus per mutua jundtis,

Ambo ætate pares, fpicis nutantibus ambo

Tempora præcinſti fubeunt : hos deinde quaterni

Ruſtica turba premunt meſſores.   Illa fonantem

Fert dextrâ citharam, terramque ad carmina pulfat.

Hi dominam agnofcunt læti, luſtrantque choreis,

* Æſtas.

Æſtivi

Æstivi veniunt terno pòst ordine Menses.

Junius impubem veris servare juventam

Visus adhuc; sicco consperfi pulvere crines,

Julius Augustusque æstu tardante sequuntur.

Tardior Augustus : quatit asper anhelitus artus.

Jam languens, jam lapsurus similisque cadenti

Ægro incessu hæret. Sudor lavit improbus ora,

Dum furit adverso malesana Canicula cælo.

Vir* subit à tergo, maturo floridus ævo,

Purpureâ fulgens zonâ fulvoque capillo.

Olli dependet promissa in pectore barba :

In nodum collecto humeros toga vestit amictu,

Flavis tincta notis, frondes imitata caducas,

Quas primum autumi decussit ab arbore frigus:

Quacunque incedit, dextrâ generofus apertâ

Spargit opes, laterique hærens telluris opimas

Multiplici fruges effundit Copia cornu.

Q 5   Sed

* Autumnus.

Sed neque fic vifus prærepti munera veris

Compenfare tamen.   Dextrâ Pomona madenti

Spumantem cratera tenens comitatur euntem.

Uvida pampineis evinctus tempora ramis

Liber adeft, curruque tigres fublimis ab alto

Flectit agens, Evæque Evæ canit orgia Bacchis.

Tum variæ comitum facies, innoxia ruris

Numina, Sileni, quos tota armenta fequuntur

Faunique, Satyrique et monticolæ Sylvani.

Proximus incedit cultu September amœno,

Dives opum, verifque novi promiffor honorum.

Illi Phœbeo facies fplendore relucet,

Aut fubitò fi quæ contriftant nubila vultum,

Mox placido abfterget rifu, cælumque ferenat.

Talis erat, talem fefe September agebat.

Protinus October, calcatis fordidus uvis,

Ingreditur pluviâque caput madefactus et auftro.

                                        Tertius

Tertius his voluit quanquam comes ire November,
Siftit fæpè gradum, atque hyemem cervice reflexâ
Refpicit inftantem tergo, et propiora tenentem.

Olli* forma fenis vergentis ad ultima vitæ
Tempora ; Sithoniæ capiti nivis æmula lucet
Canities ; baculus veftigia languida firmat.
Barba riget glacie concretis pendula cruftis ;
Frons rugofa, oculi fuffufi fanguine et igni.
Pectoribus tenus·hædinis in pellibus horret,
Hirfutâ impexus fetâ ; de crinibus urfi
Tegmen habet capiti.   Sed vis adeò afpera cæli
Frigore torpentes artus penetrârat et offa,
Ut, vifu miferum, penitus lunatus in arcum
Haud ufquam valeat cæli convexa tueri.
Ter conatus erat fe recto attollere trunco,
Ter genuum junctura fenem fruftrata labafcit,
Officiumque negat.   Pede jam titubante minatur

* Hyems.

Q 6   Succiduus

Succiduus lapfum, tantis algoribus impar,

Si non continuò focios ea cura fubiret

Suftentare manu, et greffus fulcire trementes.

Hinc graditur Comus, dapibus qui præfidet, illinc

Fati annofa Parens, magnâ quæ voce per umbras.

Ufque monet, quotquot fub iniquâ forte laborant,

Æquâ ut mente ferant, duri quodcunque ferendum eft.

Totus in afpectu Comi defixus inhæfi.

Parte fub adverfâ chlamydis, quam fulgida rubro

Purpura diftinguit limbo, fine labe renidet

Pictus acu Phrygiâ et ferrugine tinctus Iberâ.

Innumeros in fronte Sales tranfverfa tuentes,

Et Rifus, hilarefque Jocos, feftofque Lepores

Fecerat intexens vario fubtemine Pallas.

Aft averfus ubi fefe fubducere cæpit,

Heu! qualis, quantùm et mutata abeuntis imago!

Calvities fqualente caput cute turpat, et artus

Conficit informis macies. Tum picta per oras

Extremas tunicæ, paffis de more capillis

Confpicitur

Confpicitur Cædes, ftriᵉto mucrone cruenta.

Sanguineo fuccinᵉta peplo juxtà accubat Ira,

Lividaque in denfum diftorquens lumina vulgus

Sufpicio.   In medio Clamores, ebria bella

Cernere erat.   Madidos infano marte videres

Fervere convivas, vinoque rubefcere menfas.

Hinc Lapithæ ftabant, genus hinc deforme, bimembres

Prælia Centauri mifcent.   Jam fraᵉta per auras

Poc‧la craterefque volant.   Furor arma miniftrat,

Immixto tellus vinoque et fanguine manat.

Tam fœdum afpeᵉtu fcelus averfatus et arma

Impia, converfo Saturnum lumine cerno.

Ille è confpeᵉtu fenfim fubrepere pergit

Furtivo taciturnus paffu : armatur aduncâ

Deᵡtram falce manum ; de lævâ clepfydra pendet.

Proxima Saturno fpatio dein Vefta reliᵉto

Adveni. æ ‧‧‧‧‧m jervans penetraiibus ig ‧m.

Dextrâ ardet lampas, dulci quam femper olivo

Flamma perennis alit. Tum turbidus imbre December,

                                        Janu‧que

Janufque et Februus veftiti pellibus omnes

Ordine fuccedunt.   Facies non omnibus una,

Nec diverfa tamen, nifi quò propiore fequentis

Quifque fibi fpatio fentit veftigia veris,

Aut levat aut denfat contractæ nubila frontis.

THE

THE

PASTORALS

OF

MR. POPE.

DONE INTO LATIN VERSE.

SPRING; or, DAMON.

The FIRST PASTORAL.

To SIR WILLIAM TRUMBAL.

FIRST in thefe fields I try the fylvan ftrains,
Nor blufh to fport on Windfor's blifsful plains.
Fair Thames, flow gently from thy facred fpring,
While on thy banks Sicilian Mufes fing,
Let vernal airs thro' trembling ofiers play,
And Albion's cliffs refound the rural lay.

You, that too wife for pride, too good for pow'r,
Enjoy the glory to be great no more;
And carrying with you all the world can boaft,
To all the world illuftrioufly are loft !

O let

VER, SIVE DAMON.

ECLOGA PRIMA.

———

Hic primùm agreſti tentavit arundine carmen,
Noſtra nec erubuit campos celebrare Camœna
Windſorios : leni, Thameſis Pater, agmine fluctus
Volve, tuo Siculæ cantant in littore Muſæ.
Per ſalices ludat tremulo verna aura ſuſurro,
Albenteſque ferant rupes ad ſidera cantus.

O qui Regum apice, & popularibus altior auris,
Oblatas ſpernis pompas, faſceſque ſuperbos
Ruris amans, aulæque & opes, ſtrepitumque relinquis
Transfuga non humilis, tenui mea carmen avenâ

Muſa

O let my Mufe her flender reed infpire,
Till in your native fhades you tune the lyre.
So when the Nightingale to reft removes,
The Thrufh may chaunt to the forfaken groves,
But charm'd to filence, liftens while fhe fings,
And all th' aërial àudience clap their wings.

Soon as the flocks fhook off the nightly dews,
Two fwains, whom Love kept wakeful and the Mufe
Po ir'd o'er the whit'ning vale their fleecy care,
Frefh as the morn, and as the feafon fair.
The dawn now blufhing on the mountain's fide,
Thus Daphnis fpoke, and Strephon thus replied.

DAPHNIS.

Hear, how the birds, on ev'ry bloomy fpray,
With joyous mufic wake the dawning day !

Why

Mufa canat, patrio donec tu lentus in arvo,

Majori moveas refonantiâ pectine fila.

Sic, ubi fub ramo captat philomela quietem,

Sylveftri merulæ nemora inter fola canoros

Fas tentare modos : fin illa filentia rumpit,

Hæc tacet : arrectis audit fimul auribus omnis

Alituum chorus, et pennis plaudentibus aditat.

Ut pecus excuffo nocturnum à vellere rorem

Difpulerat, curis animum vigilantibus acti,

Lanigeros duxêre greges ad pafcua Daphnis

Atque bonus Strephon ; Mufâ afpirante canendo

Ambo pares, formofi annis florentibus ambo.

Jamque Aurorâ novo ftringebat lumine montes ;

Hæc Daphnis, cui fic refpondit in ordine Strephon.

DAPHNIS.

Audin' ut modulis refonant arbufta fonoris,

Nafcentemque diem genus evocat omne volucrum !

Cur

Why ſtand we mute, when early linnets ſing,

When warbling Philomel ſalutes the ſpring ?

Why ſtand we ſad, when Phoſphor ſhines ſo clear,

And laviſh Nature paints the purple year ?

STREPHON.

Sing then, and Damon ſhall attend the ſtrain,

While yon' ſlow oxen turn the furrow'd plain.

Here the bright crocus and blue vi'let glow,

Here weſtern winds on breathing roſes blow.

I'll ſtake yon' lamb, that near the fountain plays,

And from the brink his dancing ſhade ſurveys.

DAPHNIS.

And I this bowl, where wanton Ivy twines,

And ſwelling cluſters bend the curling vines.

Four figures riſing from the work appear,

The various ſeaſons of the rolling year :

And what is that, which binds the radiant ſky,

Where twelve fair ſigns in beauteous order lie ?

DAMON.

Cur taciti flamus ? Jam matutina canoros
Fundit alauda modos, jam ver Philomela falutat.
Cur mœfti ftamus? Claro jam fulget Olympo
Phofphorus, & rofeum natura redintegrat annum.

STREPHON.

Incipe ; tu Damon, certaminis arbiter efto,
Dum lenti exercent tauri fub vomere campum.
Hic crocus, & cafiæ molles, violæque renident,
Purpureæque rofæ Zephyris fpirantibus halant.
Illum ego ponam agnum, fontis qui ludit ad undas,
Ludentifque fuam de margine profpicit umbram.

DAPHNIS.

Poculum & hoc ego, cui torno fuperaddita vitis
Panditur, effufos hederâ cingente racemos ;
Anni vertentis quatuor cœlata figuris
Tempora convexis furgunt : & quid fuit illud,
Quod paribus cingit cœleftem partibus orbem,
Quà duodena æquo volvuntur tramite figna ?

DAMON.

DAMON.

Then fing by turns, by turns the Mufes fing.

Now hawthorns bloffom, now the daifies fpring,

Now leaves the trees, and flow'rs adorn the ground.

Begin; the vales fhall ev'ry note rebound.

STREPHON.

Infpire me, Phœbus, in my Delia's praife,

With Waller's ftrains, or Granville's moving lays!

A milk-white bull fhall at your altar ftand,

That threats a fight, and fpurns the rifing fand.

DAPHNIS.

Pan, let my numbers equal Strephon's lays,

Of Parian ftone thy ftatue will I raife;

But if I conquer and augment my fold,

Thy Parian ftatue fhall be changed to gold.

STREPHON.

Me gentle Delia beckons from the plain,

Then hid in fhades, eludes her eager fwain:

But

DAMON.

Alternis canite, oblectant alterna Camoenas.

Nunc pratum omne nitet, nunc omnis parturit arbor;

Frondibus & fylvæ vernant, & floribus agri.

Dicite ; vocales referent ad fidera valles.

STREPHON.

Delia mi canitur ; tu fuffice, Phœbe, canenti

Carmina Wallerii, aut Granvilli digna Cam.ænis.

Tergore candenti taurus tibi ftabit ad aras,

Qui cornu feriat, pedibufque laceffat arenam.

DAPHNIS.

Pan, mihi fi dones Strephona æquare canendo,

Ipfe tibi fignum Pario de marmore ponam.

Sin viacam, numeroque auctum mihi crefcat ovile,

Marmore pro Pario ftabis confpectus in auro.

STREPHON.

Me mea blanda vocat pellaci Delia nutu ;

Nec mora, prorumpeas denfam fe condit in umbram.

Acer

But feigns a laugh to fee me fearch around,

And by that laugh the willing fair is found.

DAPHNIS.

The fprightly Sylvia trips along the green ;

She runs, but hopes fhe does not run unfeen.

While a kind glance at her purfuer flies,

How much at variance are her feet and eyes !

STREPHON.

O'er golden fands let rich Pactolus flow,

And trees weep amber on the banks of Po,

Bleft Thames's fhores the brighteft beauties yield.

Feed here my lambs, I'll feek no diftant field.

DAPHNIS.

Celeftial Venus haunts Idalia's groves ;

Diana Cynthus, Ceres Hybla loves ;

If Windfor-fhades delight the matchlefs maid,

Cynthus and Hybla yield to Windfor-fhade.

STREPHON.

Acer amore fequor : ludit primùm illa fequentem
Improba, mox ficto gaudet fe prodere rifu.

DAPHNIS.

Sylvia gramineum celeri pede corripit arvum :
Jamque fugit, fefeque cupit fugitiva videri.
Ipfa fibi difcors fequiturque fugitque fequentem,
Dum vifu repetit, quem curfu vitat amantem.

STREPHON.

Auriferas jactet dives Pactolus arenas,
Eridani in ripis fudent electra myricæ ;
Blandiùs arrident Thamifino in littore campi :
Parcite, oves, procedere ; veftra hæc pafcua funto.

DAPHNIS.

Diligit Idaliæ facros Venus aurea lucos ;
Hybla fragrans Cereri, Dianæ Cynthus amatur.
Windforios habitet tantùm mea Sylvia campos,
Windforiis cedent campis & Cynthus & Hybla.

R   *STREPHON.*

STREPHON.

All nature mourns, the fkies relent in fhow'rs,
Hufh'd are the birds, and clofed the drooping flow'rs,
If Delia fmile, the flow'rs begin to fpring,
The fkies to brighten, and the birds to fing.

DAPHNIS.

All nature laughs, the groves are frefh and fair,
The Sun's mild luftre warms the vital air ;
If Sylvia fmiles, new glories gild the fhore,
And vanquifh'd nature feems to charm no more.

STREPHON.

In fpring the fields, in autumn hills I love,
At morn the plains, at noon the fhady grove,
But Delia always ; abfent from her fight,
Nor plains at morn, nor groves at noon delight.

DAPHNIS.

Sylvia's like autumn ripe, yet mild as May,
More bright than noon, yet frefh as early day.

Ev'n

STREPHON.

Omnia nunc fqualent; contriftant æthera nimbi,

Trifte filent volucres; languet flos omnis in agro;

Delia fi ridet, fugiunt vaga nubila cœlo,

Flora redit, gaudentque choros renovare volucres.

DAPHNIS.

Omnia nunc florent, nunc formofiffima latè

Sylva viret; placidis mitefcunt folibus auræ:

Sylvia fi ridet, decorat lux altera campos,

Et natura novo fuperata rubefcit honore.

STREPHON.

Vere novo valles, autumno tempore montes,

Mane juvant agri, mediis fub folibus umbræ,

Delia me femper; fin illa abfcefferit, agri

Nec me mane juvant, mediis nec folibus umbræ.

DAPHNIS.

Veris & autumni fibi Sylvia jungit honores;

Pulchrior autumno eft, & vernâ fuavior aurâ.

R 2   Montibus

Ev'n fpring difpleafes, when fhe fhines not here,

But bleft with her, 'tis fpring throughout the year.

STREPHON.

Say, Daphnis, fay, in what glad foil appears

A wond'rous tree, that facred Monarchs bears:

Tell me but this, and I'll difclaim the prize,

And give the conqueft to thy Sylvia's eyes.

DAPHNIS.

Nay tell me firft, in what more happy fields

The Thiftle fprings, to which the Lily yields:

And then a nobler prize I will refign;

For Sylvia, charming Sylvia fhall be thine.

DAMON.

Ceafe to contend; for, Daphnis, I decree,

The bowl to Strephon, and the lamb to thee.

Bleft fwains, whofe Nymphs in ev'ry grace excel,

Bleft Nymphs, whofe fwains thofe graces fing fo well!

Now

Montibus his nostris abeat, ver displicet ; ipsâ
Præsenti, felix toto ver regnat in anno.

STREPHON.

Dic, quibus in terris ramis felicibus arbor
Sacratos gestat Reges ; tum, lite repostâ,
Haud sanè abnuero pateram tibi victus, & agnum
Tradere : parto ibit tua Sylvia læta triumpho.

DAPHNIS.

Dic, quibus ipse prior melioribus exit in agris
Carduus assurgens, cui lactea lilia cedunt :
Tum tu nobilius referes, me dante, trophæum :
Sylvia ducetur tibi candida sponsa marito.

DAMON.

Sistite, jam pueri ; tibi sinum adjudico, Strephon,
Et tibi, Daphni, agnum.   Vos an magis arte canendi
Felices, pueri, an pulchro vos corpore, Nymphæ ?
Felices, pueri ; felices vos quoque, Nymphæ.

Surgite

Now rife, and hafte to yonder woodbine bow'rs,

A foft retreat from fudden vernal fhow'rs ;

The turf with rural dainties fhall be crown'd,

While op'ning blooms diffufe their fweets around.

For fee, the gath'ring flocks to fhelter tend,

And from the Pleiads fruitful fhow'rs defcend.

SUMMER ;

Surgite nunc adeò, quodque hîc propè frondet, ad
    antrum

Tendite, fecurum verno tutamen ab imbre.

Graminex luxu menfæ fternentur agrefti,

Floriferumque nemus fuaves diffundet odores.

Namque videtis, uti pecudes ad ovilia tendunt,

Fœcundoque graves defcendunt Pleiades imbre.

ÆSTAS;

SUMMER; or, ALEXIS.

THE SECOND PASTORAL.

To Dr. GARTH.

A SHEPHERD's Boy, he feeks no better name,
Led forth his flocks along the filver Thame,
Where dancing funbeams on the waters play'd,
And verdant alders form'd a quiv'ring fhade.
Soft as he mourn'd, the ftreams forgot to flow,
The flocks around a dumb compaffion fhow,
The Naïds wept in ev'ry wat'ry bow'r,
And Jove confented in a filent fhow'r.

Accept

ÆSTAS, sive ALEXIS.

ECLOGA II.

PASTORIS famulus, nec enim fibi majus Alexis

Nomen avet, fœcunda greges ad pafcua juffit

Tendere, quà placido Thamifis fecat arva fluento.

Mite repercuffi folis jubar errat in undis,

Et tremulam faciunt alni paftoribus umbram.

Dum dulcè hîc queritur, dum carmina fundit ad auras,

Stant mœftæ pecudes circùm, & fufpenfa quiefcunt

Flumina : Näiades liquidis flevêre fub antris,

Flevit & irriguo defcendens Jupiter imbre.

R 5 Accipe

Accept, O GARTH, the Mufe's early lays,
That adds this wreath of ivy to thy bays ;
Hear what from love unpractifed hearts endure,
From love, the fole difeafe thou can'ft not cure.

Ye fhady beeches, and ye cooling ftreams,
Defence from Phœbus', not from Cupid's beams,
To you I mourn ; nor to the deaf I fing ;
The woods fhall anfwer, and their echo ring.
The hills and rocks attend my doleful lay,
Why art thou prouder, and more hard than they ?
The bleating fheep with my complaints agree ?
They parch'd with heat, and I inflamed by thee.
The fultry Sirius burns the thirfty plains,
While in thy heart eternal winter reigns.

Where ftray, ye Mufes, in what lawn or grove,
While your Alexis pines in hopelefs love ?

In

Accipe, GARTHA, novo deductum pectine carmen,
Accipe, quamque ferunt mufæ, fine tempora circum
Inter Apollineas hederam tibi ferpere lauros.
En, quid amor, tibi amor folum infanabile, cogit
Ferre, quibufque premit juvenilia pectora curis.

Vos, gelidi fontes, fagi, vos teftor, opacæ,
Quæ radios Phœbi, non ignem arcetis Amoris,
Quas dolor effundit, juftas audite querelas.
Non canimus furdis ; refpondent flebilè fylvæ,
Flebilè clivofi montes, & faxa reclamant.
Durior heu quianam faxis, Amarylli, canentem
Refpuis, & nullas voces tractabilis audis ?
Flebilè balantes refpondent quæftibus agni ;
Illos ficca dies, tu me, meus ignis, aduris.
Æftifer accendit fitientes Sirius agros,
At tibi perpetuâ frigent præcordia brumâ.

Quæ nemora, aut qui vos faltus habuêre, Camœnæ,
Vefter Alexis ubi ftudio tabebat inani ?

R 6

An

In thofe fair fields, where facred Ifis glides,

Or elfe where Cam his winding vales divides?

As in the cryftal fpring I view my face,

Frefh rifiug blufhes paint the wat'ry glafs.

But fince thofe graces pleafe thy eyes no more,

I fhun the fountains, which I fought before.

Once I was fkill'd in ev'ry herb that grew,

And ev'ry plant, that drinks the morning dew.

Ah wretched fhepherd, what avails thy art,

To cure thy lambs, but not to heal thy heart!

Let other fwains attend the rural care,

Feed fairer flocks, or richer fleeces fheer.

But nigh yon' mountain let me tune my lays,

Embrace my Love; and bind my brows with bays.

That flute is mine, which Colin's tuneful breath

Infpir'd when living, and bequeath'd in death.

He faid; Alexis, take this pipe, the fame

That taught the groves my Rofalinda's name:

But

An quà pulcher Iſis leni rigat agmine campos,

An quà per valles ſinuat ſua flumina Camus ?

Nuper ego lucentis aquæ me in margine vidi ;

Suavè rubeſcentem mihi rettulit unda figuram.

Sed cùm noſtræ adeò formæ tibi ſordet imago,

Ipſe ego jam fontes, modò qui placuêre, relinquo.

Quæ procul in ſylvis plantæ naſcuntur, & omnes

Virtutes herbarum nôram, uſumque medendi.

Hei mihi ! quid prodeſt plantas noviſſe, vel herbas,

Si crudelis amor nullâ eſt medicabilis arte,

Nec mihi, quæ gregibus, medicantia gramina proſunt !

Formoſos alii per mollia paſcua ducant

Auſpicio meliore greges, & vellera mutent ;

Me juvat umbroſo tecum hoc ſub monte jacentem

Et canere, & viridi præcingere tempora lauro.

Eſt mihi, quam Corydon modulans inflare ſolebat,

Fiſtula ; ſupremum hoc, inquit, morientis, Alexi,

Munus habe ; hæc nomen Roſalindæ rura docebat.

Sic

But now the reeds fhall hang on yonder tree,
For ever filent, fince defpifed by thee.

And yet my numbers pleafe the rural throng,
Rough Satyrs dance, and Pan applauds the fong.
The Nymphs, forfaking ev'ry cave and fpring,
Their early fruit, and milk-white turtles bring.
Each am'rous Nymph prefers her gifts in vain,
On you their gifts are all beftow'd again.
For you the fwains the faireft flow'rs defign;
And in one garland all their beauties join.
Accept the wreath, which you deferve alone,
In whom all beauties are comprifed in one.

See, what delights in fylvan fcenes appear!
Defcending Gods have found Elyfium here.
In woods bright Venus with Adonis ftray'd,
And chafte Diana haunts the foreft fhade.
Come, fprightly nymph, and blefs the filent hours,
When fwains from fheering feek their nightly bow'rs;

When

Sic Corydon; fed jam pendebit ab arbore buxus
Ufque filens, cùm noftra adeò tibi carmina fordent.

Sæpè tamen plaufus mihi ruftica turba canenti,
Panque Deus, Satyrique leves, Faunique dedêre.
Ipfæ etiam Nymphæ fylvis venêre reliétis. .
Primitias ultrò frugum, niveafque palumbes
Quas tibi fervo, ferunt. ⸱ Studiis certantibus omnes
Paftores tibi ferta parant : tibi Flora renidens
Purpureos neétit ruris redolentis honores.
Quin ergo, quam fola meres, Amarylli, coronam
Accipe : nam campis, nam tu decus omne colonis.

Afpice, quanta tenet fylveftria rura voluptas ? ·
Æthere delapfi coluerunt Dii quoque fylvas.
Pulchra Venus fylvis cum pulchro errabat Adoni,
Atque Diana frequens virides amat incola faltus.
Nympha, veni : præfente volat te gratiòr hora,
Cùm tonfis redeunt ovibus fub noéte coloni;

Cum

When weary reapers quit the fultry field,

And crown'd with corn their thanks to Ceres yield.

This harmlefs grove no lurking viper hides,

But in my breaft the ferpent Love abides.

Here bees from bloffoms fip the rofy dew,

But your Alexis knows no fweets but you.

Oh! deign to vifit our forfaken feats,

The moffy fountains and the green retreats!

Where'er you walk, cool gales fhall fan the glade,

Trees, where you fit, fhall croud into a fhade:

Where'er you tread, the blufhing flow'rs fhall rife,

And all things flourifh, where you turn your eyes.

Oh! how I long with you to pafs my days,

Invoke the Mufes, and refound your praife!

Your praife the birds fhall chant in ev'ry grove,

And winds fhall waft it to the pow'rs above.

But would you fing, and rival Orpheus' ftrain,

The wond'ring forefts foon fhould dance again,

The moving mountains hear the pow'rful call,

And headlong ftreams hang lift'ning in their fall.

But

Cum vincti ex agro meſſores tempora ſpicis

Adſunt, & Cererem feſto clamore ſalutant.

Squameus hîc tacitâ nullus latet anguis in herbâ,

Sed mihi amor latitans nutrit ſub corde venenum.

Hîc roſeos populantur apes, ſua gaudia, flores;

Nulla abſente tuus te gaudia novit Alexis.

O! precor, ô! noſtras dignare inviſere ſedes,

Et virides muſco fontes, nemorumque receſſus.

Quacumque incedas, ſpirante favonius aurâ

Apricos recreabit agros: ubicumque ſedentem

Sylva ſequax denſâ ramorum proteget umbrâ.

Sub pedibus mollem ſternet tibi Flora tapetem,

Quàque feras oculos, rerum nova gloria ſurget.

O dulces liceat tecum mihi ducere ſoles,

Aonioque tuas percurrere pectine laudes!

Te volucrum per rura chori, te campus, & omnis

Sylva canet, nomenque ferent ad ſidera venti.

Sin certare voles, Orpheumque æquare canendo,

In numerum rurſus ſylvaſque umbraſque videbis

Ludere, & excelſos motare cacumina montes,

Auritoſque trahi ſuſpenſis lapſibus amnes.

Sed

But fee, the fhepherds fhun the noon-day heat,
The lowing herds to murm'ring brooks retreat,
To clofer fhades the panting flocks remove.
Ye Gods, and is there no relief for Love?

But foon the fun with milder rays defcends
To the cool ocean, where his journey ends:
On me Love's fiercer flames for ever prey,
By night he fcorches, as he burns by day.

AUTUMN;

Sed viden! è medio sol igneus ardet Olympo,

Et fessæ pecudes frigus sectantur opacum.

Cum grege pastores umbras & flumina quærunt:

Hei mihi, quòd duro nullum est solamen amori!

Mox cœlum emensus, sol æquore tinget anhelos

Pronus equos, ponetque viæ finemque labori:

Me tamen usque novis violentior æstibus urit

Ignis, & ardentem noctesque diesque fatigat.

AUTUMNUS,

AUTUMN; or, HYLAS and ÆGON.

THE THIRD PASTORAL.

To Mr. WYCHERLEY.

BENEATH the shade a spreading beech displays
Hylas and Ægon sung their rural lays.
This mourn'd a faithless, that an absent Love,
And Delia's name and Doris' fill'd the grove.

Ye Mantuan Nymphs, your sacred succour bring
Hylas and Ægon's rural lays I sing.

Thou, whom the Nine with Plautus' wit inspire,
The art of Terence, and Menander's fire;

Whose

AUTUMNUS, sive HYLAS et ÆGON.

ECLOGA III.

FORTE' fub umbrofo frondentis tegmine fagi
Pulcher Hylas, pulcherque unà confederat Ægon.
Hic infidum, ille abfentem deflebat amorem,
Deliaque & Doris nemorofa per arva fonabant.

Andinæ Mufæ, facros recludite fontes;
Sollicitos Ægonis Hylæque canemus amores.

O, cui Pierides numeros, artemque Terentî,
Plautinofque dedêre fales, ignefque Menandri;

O tu,

Whofe fenfe inftructs us, and whofe humour charms,
Whofe judgment fways us, and whofe fpirit warms;
Oh, fkill'd in nature, fee the hearts of fwains,
Their artlefs paffions, and their tender pains.

Now fetting Phœbus fhone fe e)ely bright,
And fleecy clouds were ftreak'd wi;h purple light,
When tuneful Hylas with melodious moan,
Taught rocks to weep, and made the mountains groan

Go, gentle gales, and bear my fighs away !
To Doris' ear the tender notes convey.
As fome fad turtle his loft Love deplores,
And with deep murmurs fills thei ounding fhores ;
Thus, far from Doris, to the winds I mourn,
Alike, unheard, unpity'd, and forlorn.

Go, gentle gales, and bear my fighs along !
For her the feather'd quires neglect their fong ;

For

O tu, qui mores hominum formare monendo

Cenfor amas, vitæque doces præcepta beatæ ;

Afpice nos, noftramque, licèt fit ruftica, Mufam,

Paftorumque bonus molles ne fperne querelas.

Jam rofeis Sol pronus equis vergebat in æquor,

Sparfaque puniceâ radiabant nubila luce ;

Argutâ cùm triftis Hylas fic cœpit avenâ,

Montefque & fcopulos Dorin refonare docebat.

Ferte meas, venti, hinc ad Dorida ferte querelas !

Scilicet ut mœrens, amifsâ conjuge, turtur

Raucà gemens gravibus latè loca quæftibus implet ;

Sic mea dum Doris procul his fejungitur arvis,

Solus, inops, expes fingultibus aftra laceffo.

Ferte meas, venti, hinc ad Dorida ferte querelas !

Illà abfente, choros mœftæ abrupêre volucres ;

Illâ

For her the limes their pleafing fhades deny ;

For her the lilies hang their heads and die..

Ye flow'rs, that droop, forfaken by the fpring,

Ye birds that, left by fummer, ceafe to fing.

Ye trees, that fade, when autumn heats remove,

Say, is not abfence death to thofe who love ?

Go, gentle gales, and bear my fighs away ?

Curfed be the fields, that caufe my Doris' ftay.

Fade ev'ry bloffom, wither ev'ry tree,

Die ev'ry flow'r, and perifh all but fhe.

What have I faid ? Where'er my Doris flies,

Let fpring attend, and fudden flow'rs arife ;

Let op'ning rofes knotted oaks adorn,

And liquid amber drop from ev'ry thorn.

Go, gentle gales, and bear my fighs along !

The birds fhall ceafe to tune their ev'ning fong,

The

Illâ abfente, fuam feffo negat arbutus umbram,

Marcentefque comas morientia lilia ponunt.

Lilia, quæ verno fpoliata jacetis honore,

Vos, canere oblitæ, fugiente æftate, volucres,

Vos fylvæ, autumno contaflæ frigore, teftor,

Longa mori fi non abfentia cogat amantem.

Ferte meas, venti, hinc ad Dorida ferte querelas!

Deteftata mihi, procul hoc quæ rure morantem

Dorin terra tenet.   Modò te mihi fofpite, Dori,

Pratorum fpolietur honos, elangueat omnis

Arbor, & in medio marcefcat flofculus arvo.

Quæ demens quæ ftulta loquor? Quofcumque pererrat

Illa locos, per prata recens comitetur euntem

Veris honos, furgant violæ, decoretur odoris

Dura rofis ilex, manentque eleflra vepretis.

Ferte meas, venti, hinc ad Dorida ferte querelas!

Antè loquax iterare modos ceffabit Aëdon,

S   Antè

The woods to move, the vagrant winds to blow,
And ſtreams to murmur, e'er my tears to flow.
Not bubbling fountains to the thirſty ſwain,
Not balmy ſleep to lab'rers faint with pain,
Not ſhow'rs to larks, or ſhun-ſhine to the bee,
Are half ſo charming, as thy ſight to me.

Go, gentle gales, and bear my ſighs away!
Come, Doris, come: ah, why this long delay?
Thro' rocks and caves the name of Doris ſounds,
Doris each cave and echoing rock rebounds.
Ye pow'rs, what pleaſing frenzy ſooths my mind?
Do lovers dream, or is my Doris kind?
She comes, my Doris comes! Now ceaſe, my lay,
And ceaſe, ye gales, to bear my ſighs away!

Next Ægon ſung, while Windſor groves admired;
Rehearſe, ye Muſes, what yourſelves inſpired.

Reſound,

Antè fufurrantes motare cacumina fylvæ,

Aut fpirare noti, aut dulci cum murmure rivi

Serpere, quàm triftes mea lumina fundere fletûs.

Non fitientem adeò fontanæ copia lymphæ

Juverit agricolam, non feffum fomnus in herbâ;

Non tam dulce apibus folis jubar, imber alaudis,

Quàm tua grata mihi veniat præfentia, Dori.

Ferte meas, venti, hinc ad Dorida ferte querelas!

Huc, ô Dori, veni; quæ te tam lenta moratur

Segnities? Te faxa vocant, collefque fupini,

Te refonæ valles, te noftræ, Dori, myricæ.

Quæ, fuperi, quæ me jucunda infania ludit?

An venit? An fingunt ipfi fibi fomnia amantes?

Doris adeft, mea Doris adeft. Jam fiftite, venti,

Siftite, nec noftras ad Dorida ferte querelas!

Vos, quæ rettulerit, fylvis mirantibus, Ægon,

Dicite, Pierides; nam vos docuiftis & illa.

S 2 Reddite

Refound, ye hills, refound my mournful ſtrain !

Of perjured Delia dying I complain.

Here, where the mountains, leſs'ning as they riſe,

Loſe the low vales, and ſteal into the ſkies ;

While lab'ring oxen, ſpent with toil and heat,

In their looſe traces from the field retreat,

While curling ſmokes from village tops are ſeen,

And the fleet ſhades glide o'er the duſky green.

Refound, ye hills, refound my mournful lay !

Beneath yon' poplar oft' we paſs'd the day :

Oft' on the rind I carved our mutual vows,

While ſhe with garlands hung the bending boughs.

The garlands fade, the rind is worn away ;

So die her vows, and ſo my hopes decay.

Refound, ye hills, refound my mournful ſtrain !

Now bright Arcturus glads the teeming grain,

Now g. en fruits on loaded branches ſhine,

And grate. cluſters ſwell with floods of wine.

Now

Reddite lugubres, cava culmina, reddite cantus!
Hìc, quà demiſſis ſeſe ſubducere ſenſim
Vallibus incipiunt, abeuntque in nubila montes,
Delia, te moriens, te, perfida Delia, teſtor.
Jam collo ex arvis redeunt languente juvenci,
Inverſique domum referunt grave pondus aratri ;
Jam procul undantem villarum culmina ad auras
Exhalant fumum, valleſque.umbrantur opacæ.

Reddite lugubres, cava culmina, reddite cantus.
Sæpè diem longo tecum ſermone ſub umbrâ
Populeâ fregi, viridique in cortice vota
Incidi, dum tu curvatis pendula ramis
Serta dabas : ſed jam poſuerunt marcida fluxum
Serta decus, fiſſo pereunt in cortice vota.
Sic fugitivus amor, ſic me ſpes luſit amantem !

Reddite lugubres, cava culmina, reddite cantus!
Jam faciunt lætas Arcturi ſidera fruges :
Jam gravidos onerant ramos poma aurea, & uvæ
Purpureo paſſim per colles nectare turgent ;

Now blufhing berries paint the yellow grove.

Juft Gods! fhall all things yield returns, but love?

Refound, ye hills, refound my mournful lay!

The fhepherds cry, " Thy flocks are left a prey."

Ah! what avails it me, the flocks to keep,

Who loft my heart, while I preferved my fheep?

Pan came, and afk'd, what magic caufed my fmart,

Or what ill eyes malignant glances dart?

What eyes but her's, alas! have pow'r to move?

Or is there magic, but what dwells in love?

Refound, ye hills, refound my mournful ftrains!

I'll fly from fhepherds, flocks, and flow'ry plains.

From fhepherds, flocks and plains, I may remove,

Forfake mankind and all the world—but love!

I know thee, Love; on foreign mountains bred,

Wolves gave thee fuck, and favage tigers fed.

Thou wert from Ætna's burning entrails torn,

Got by fierce whirlwinds, and in thunder born.

Refound

Ditia flaventes pingunt aviaria baccæ.

Tanquam hæc decepti mihi fint folamen amoris !

Reddite lugubres, cava culmina, reddite cantus !

Paftores clamant, " Tibi oves abiguntur & hædi."

Hei mihi ! quid prodeft vel oves fervâffe vel hædos,

Si dum fervo gregem, pereo mifer ipfe ? Lycæi

Arcadii venit Deus ; ecqua venefica, dixit,

Te vidit, fanofque avertit peftore fenfus ?

Sola mihi fanos avertit Delia fenfus.

Unus amor mifero mentem mihi fafcinat omncm.

Reddite lugubres, cava culmina, reddite cantus !

Ibo, & paftores, pecudefque, & amœna vireta

Linquam : at paftores, pecudefque & amœna vireta

Linquere quid juvat, infano nifi linquar amore ?

Nunc fcio, quid fit Amor : duris in montibus ortum

Nutrivêre lupæ, & tigres pavêre rapaces.

Illum è vifceribus vulfum flagrantibus Ætnæ

Turbo nigras fudit, cœlo indignante, fub auras.

Refound, ye hills, refound my mournful lay !
Farewel, ye woods, adieu the light of day !
One leap from yonder cliff fhall end my pains.
No more, ye hills, no more refound my ftrains !

    Thus fung the fhepherds, till th' approach of night,
The fkies yet blufhing with departing light ;
When falling dews with fpangles deck'd the glade,
And the low fun had lengthen'd ev'ry fhade.

WINTER ;

Reddite lugubres, cava culmina, reddite cantus!

Sylva vale dilecta, vale, lux alma diei!

Istius aërio præceps de vertice rupis

Deferar; ille modus fuerit finisque dolori.

Reddere lugubres, cava culmina, parcite cantus!

Talia jactabant, cùm jam procedere vesper

Cœperat, & roseum suffundere lumen Olympo.

Humida jam vitreis rorabant gramina guttis,

Solque cadens rerum crescentes auxerat umbras.

HYEMS,

WINTER; OR, DAPHNE.

THE FOURTH PASTORAL.

To the MEMORY of Mrs. TEMPEST.

LYCIDAS.

THYRSIS, the mufic of that murm'ring fpring
Is not fo mournful, as the ftrains you fing.
Nor rivers winding thro' the vales below,
So fweetly warble, or fo fmoothly flow.
Now fleeping flocks on their foft fleeces lie,
The moon, ferene in glory, mounts the fky.
While filent birds forget their tuneful lays,
Oh fing of Daphne's fate, and Daphne's praife!

THYRSIS.

Behold the groves, that fhine with filver froft,
Their beauty wither'd, and their verdure loft.

Here

HYEMS, SIVE DAPHNE.

ECLOGA IV.

LYCIDAS.

NON tam triſtè ſonat trepidans per gramina rivus,

Quàm mihi, Thyrſi, tuâ modulatum carmen avenâ :

Nec riguas inter labentïa flumina valles

Tam blandùm, tam dulcè fluunt.   Jam vellere molli

Suffultæ pecudes placidæ dant membra quieti.

Candida conſcendit cœlum face luna ſerenâ,

Et modulos oblita ſilet gens alma volucrum.

Incipe ; crudeli præreptam funere Daphnen

Dicamus ; dicenda neget quis carmina Daphnæ ?

THYRSIS.

Aſpice, ut excuſſo capitis frondentis honore

Marcet iners, gelidiſque albet nemus omne pruiniɔ.

S 6.   Hic

Here fhall I try the fweet Alexis' ftrain,
That call'd the lift'ning Dryads to the plain?
Thames heard the numbers, as he flow'd along,
And bade his willows learn the moving fong.

LYCIDAS.

So may kind rains their vital moifture yield,
And fwell the future harveft of the field!
Begin; this charge the dying Daphne gave,
And faid, "Ye fhepherds, fing around my grave!"
Sing, while befide the fhaded tomb I mourn,
And with frefh bays her rural fhrine adorn.

THYRSIS.

Ye gentle Mufes, leave your chryftal fpring,
Let Nymphs and Sylvans cyprefs garlands bring.
Ye weeping Loves, the ftream with myrtles hide,
And break your bows, as when Adonis died:
And with your golden darts, now ufelefs grown,
Infcribe a verfe on this relenting ftone:

"Let

Hìc ego, quæ dulci teſtudine luſit Alexis,

Carmina tentârim, Dryadas queis ille ſequentes

Montibus elicuit ? Stratis æqualiter undis

Audiit hæc Thamiſis, ſalicefque edifcere juſſit.

LYCIDAS.

Sic pluviis fœcundus aquis ſata nutriat humor,

Et lætos faciat venturis meſſibus auctus !

Incipe ; ſic Daphne moriens mandavit, & inquit,

" Carminibus tumulum memores luſtrate, coloni !

Incipe, ego triſti dum munere functus, agreſtem

Arbuteis tumulum virgis & vimine texo.

THYRSIS.

Vos, ô Caſtalides, ſacratos linquite fontes,

Et Satyri, & Nymphæ, ferali texta cupreſſo

Serta date. O, lachrymis quis enim modus adſit ?

    Amores

Idalii, mœſtâ fontes obducite myrto ;

Frangite nunc arcus, nam ſic fleviſtis Adonin.

Nunc nudas deponite, inania tela, ſagittas,

Cuſpide vel verſâ tumulo hoc infcribite carmen :

" Let nature change, let heav'n and earth deplore,
" Fair Daphne 's dead, and love is now no more!"

'Tis done, and nature's various charms decay:
See, gloomy clouds obfcure the chearful day!
Now hung with pearls the dropping trees appear,
Their faded honours fcatter'd on her bier.
See, where on earth the flow'ry glories lie,
With her they flourifh'd, and with her they die.
Ah! what avail the beauties nature wore?
Fair Daphne 's dead, and beauty is no more!

For her the flocks refufe their verdant food,
The thirfty heifers fhun the gliding flood,
The filver fwans her haplefs fate bemoan,
In notes more fad, than when they fing their own.
In hollow caves fweet Echo filent lies,
Silent, or only to her name replies:
Her name with pleafure once fhe taught the fhore.
Now Daphne 's dead, and pleafure is no more!

No.

" Se mutet natura, folumque & fidera plorent,

" Pulchra perit Daphne, perit omnis gratia amorum !

Sic placitum ; natura anni languentis honores

Mutat, & obfcurum contriftant nubila cœlum.

Illachrymat mœftùm guttis ftillantibus arbor,

Avulfifque comis fpargit lugubre feretrum.

Heu ! lapfus periit, Daphne pereunte, virentis

Ruris honor : nituiffe juvat quid floribus arva ?

Pulchra perit Daphne, perit omnis gratia florum !

Vi&a dolore pecus viridantibus abftinet herbis,

Nec meminit quadrupes attingere fluminis undam ;

Albentes cycni Daphnen flevêre, nec unquam

Tam dulci extremam linguâ cecinêre querelam,

Cum fua fata vocant : mœftum caput abdita fylvis

Aut filet, aut Daphnen plangentibus affonat Echo.

Illa fuam nuper Daphnen, ea fola voluptas,

Littoris incurvi fcopulos refonare docebat ;

Nunc omnis periit, Daphne pereunte, voluptas !

Non

No grateful dews defcend from ev'ning fkies,

No morning odours from the flow'rs arife ;

No rich perfumes refrefh the fruitful field,

Nor fragrant herbs their native incenfe yield.

The balmy Zephyrs, filent fince her death,

Lament the ceafing of a fweeter breath ;

Th' induftrious bees neglect their golden ftore.

Fair Daphne 's dead, and fweetnefs is no more !

No more the mounting larks, while Daphne fings,

Shall lift'ning in mid air fufpend their wings.

No more the birds fhall imitate her lays,

Or hufh'd with wonder, hearken from the fprays ;

No more the ftreams their murmurs fhall forbear,

A fweeter mufic than their own to hear,

But tell the reeds, and tell the vocal fhore,

Fair Daphne's dead, and mufic is no more !

Her fate is whifper'd by the gentle breeze,

And told in fighs to all the trembling trees ;

The .

Non jam nocturni descendunt æthere rores,

Non Zephyro flores spirant, non floribus agri,

Nec soliti campis herbarum afflantur odores.

Triste silens Zephyrus, Daphne, tua funera deflet,

Dulcior heu Zephyris Daphne, dum vita manebat!

Oblitæ jam ruris, apes se in tecta recondunt,

Nec liquido curant distendere nectare cellas.

Pulchra perit Daphne, perit omnis gloria mellis!

Non ultrà attonitæ, Daphne dum cantat, alaudæ

In medio celeres suspendent aëre pennas.

Non numeros mirata dehinc Philomela canentis

Audiet, aut similes imitabitur æmula cantus.

Non aurita prement lapsus jam flumina, Daphnes

Auditura modos & non imitabile carmen.

Flebilè sed junci, sed flebilè ripa sonabunt.

Pulchra perit Daphne, perit omnis gratia cantûs!

Heu fatum crudele! gravi nemus omne susurro

Ingeminat; Daphnes fatum sub vallibus imis

Sylva

The trembling trees, in ev'ry plain and wood,

Her fate remurmur to the filver flood ;

The filver flood, fo lately calm, appears

Swell'd with new paffion; and o'erflows with tears.

The winds, and trees and floods her death deplore,

Daphne, our grief, our glory now no more !

But fee ! where Daphne woud'ring mounts on high

Above the clouds, above the ftarry fky !

Eternal beauties grace the fhining fcene,

Fields ever frefh, and groves for ever green.

There, while you reft in Amaranthine bow'rs,

Or from thofe meads felect unfading flow'rs,

Behold us kindly, who your name implore,

Daphne, our Goddefs, and our grief no more !

LYCIDAS.

How all things liften, while thy Mufe complains !

Such filence waits on Philomela's ftrains,

In

Sylva gemit, gemitufque ferunt ad flumina valles.

Flumina, quæ nuper leni labentia rivo

Stringebant ripas, magno nunc turbida motu

Volvuntur, fternuntque fretis undantibus arva.

Te, fylvæ, te auftri, te, Daphne, flumina plorant ;

Heu fuperas, Daphne, nunquam reditura fub auras!

Sed viden ! æthereos Daphne fuperevolat orbes,

Miraturque infrà ftellafque & nubila volvi.

Hîc cœlefte folum, hîc facies lætiffima rerum

Semper, & æterno viridantes gramine campi.

Seu tu prata tenes Amarantho umbrata recenti,

Seu legis ufque novós formofo pollice flores,

Afpice nos, rebufque veni non afpera noftris,

Tu Dea, tu Daphne, votis jam affueta vocari,

Nec lachrymis ultrà mœftifve urgenda querelis.

LYCIDAS.

Ut tranquilla filent loca cuncta, ftupentque canentem!

Sic, labente die, Philomela filentia mulcet,

Dum

In fome ftill ev'ning, when the whifp'ring breeze
Pants on the leaves, and dies upon the trees.
To thee, bright Goddefs, oft' a lamb fhall bleed,
If teeming ewes increafe my fleecy breed.
While plants their fhade, or flow'rs their odours give
Thy name, thy honour, and thy praife fhall live!

THYRSIS.

But fee, Orion fheds unwholefome dews.
Arife, the pines a noxious fhade diffufe.
Sharp Boreas blows, and Nature feels decay.
Time conquers all, and we muft time obey.
Adieu, ye vales, ye mountains, ftreams and groves,
Adieu, ye fhepherds, rural lays and loves;
Adieu, my flocks; farewel, ye fylvan crew;
Daphne, farewel; and all the world adieu!

THE

Dum placido Zephyrus per fylvam fibilat ore

Leniter afpirans, & ventilat aëre frondes.

O Dea, fæpè tibi teneram maĉtabimus agnam,

Si fœtura gregem pleno fuppleverit anno.

Sic umbras dum fylva dabit, dum Chloris odores,

Noftra eris, æternùm noftris celebrabere faftis.

THYRSIS.

Sed jam lethiferos rores diffundit Orion.

Surgamus ; pini gravis eft cantantibus umbra.

Sævit atrox boreas, fentit natura feneĉtam.

Omnia fert ætas, breve & infuperabile tempus

Omnibus eft vitæ. Felices vivite campi,

Vivite flumineæ valles, montefque fupini :

Vivite, paftores, paftorum vivite lufus.

Tu, Daphne, & quicquid vafto compleĉtitur orbe

Terra, vale ; æternùm fylvæque urbefque valete.

MESSIAS.

THE MESSIAH.

A SACRED ECLOGUE.

Ye Nymphs of Solyma, begin the fong ;
To heav'nly themes fublimer ftrains belong.
The moſſy fountains, and the fylvan ſhades,
The dreams of Pindus and th' Aonian maids
Delight no more. O thou my voice infpire,
Who touch'd Ifaiah's hallow'd lips with fire !

Rapt into future times, the Bard begun :
A Virgin ſhall conceive, a Virgin bear a Son.
From Jeſſe's root behold a branch arife,
Whofe facred flow'r with fragrance fills the ſkies.

Th'

MESSIAS.

ECLOGA SACRA.

———

BETHLEMIDES Nymphæ, cœlefte indicite
carmen.

Si canimus Numen, carmen fit Numine dignum.

Nam neque mufcofi fontes, neque fomnia Pindi,

Nam neque Pierides, fylvifque umbrata profanis.

Rura juvant. O, qui Ifaiæ facra ignibus ora

Luftrafti, Tu vocem infpira animamque canenti.

Hæc retulit vates venturi præfcius ævi.

Concipiet Virgo, pariet Virgo integra prolem.

Stirpe è Jeffæâ nafcetur virga, perenni

Flore nitens; auris redolet fragantibus æther.

Olli

Th' etherial Spirit o'er its leaves fhall move,

And on its top defcends the myftic Dove.

The fick and weak the healing plant fhall aid,

From ftorms a fhelter, and from heat a fhade.

Ye Heav'ns, from high the dewy nectar pour,

And in foft filence fhed the kindly fhow'r.

All crimes fhall ceafe, and ancient Fraud fhall fail;

Returning Juftice lift aloft her fcale;

Peace o'er the world her olive wand extend,

And white-robed innocence from heav'n defcend.

Swift fly the years, and rife th' expected morn!

O fpring to light, aufpicious Babe, be born!

See, nature haftes her earlieft wreaths to bring

With all the incenfe of the breathing fpring.

See lofty Lebanon his head advance,

See nodding forefts on the mountains dance.

See fpicy clouds from lowly Saron rife,

And Carmel's flow'ry top perfumes the fkies.

Hark,

Olli divinus per frondes lenè feretur

Spiritus, inque apicem defcendet myfticus ales.

Infirmis ægrifque mali contagia cæli

Defendet, gravidofque notos æftufque nocentes.

Defuper, ô cœli, rorantem inducite nubem,

Et lætum tacitis demittite lapfibus imbrem.

Crimina jam fugient; terras Aftræa revifet.

Fraus antiqua cadet, placidâque infignis olivâ

Pax, et cana Fides almo remeabit olympo.

Pergite feftinis procedere menfibus, anni,

Et jubar optatum terris, Aurora, reclude.

Nafcere, Dive Puer ; jam nunc tibi germine læto

Terra tumet, funditque novis munufcula cunis.

Te nemus omne vocat, te mons, te vallis, et altis

Excita fylva jugis : tibi celfa cacumina motat

Exultans Libanus.   Sacro jam fidera fumo

Lambit odoratus Saron, jam florea pandit

Munera Carmelus, fertifque virentibus halat.

T

Audin

Hark, a glad voice the lonely defert chears;

Prepare the way; a God, a God appears.

A God, a God, the vocal hills reply,

The rocks proclaim th' approaching Deity.

Lo, earth receives him from the bending fkies!

Sink down, ye mountains, and ye vallies, rife.

With heads declined, ye cedars, homage pay;

Be fmooth, ye rocks; ye rapid floods, give way.

The Saviour comes, by ancient bards foretold:

Hear him, ye deaf, and, all ye blind, behold.

He from thick films fhall purge the vifual ray,

And on the fightlefs eye-ball pour the day.

'Tis he th' obftructed paths of found fhall clear,

And bid new mufic charm th' unfolding ear.

The dumb fhall fing, the lame his crutch forego,

And leap exulting, like the bounding roe.

No figh, no murmur the wide world fhall hear,

From ev'ry face he wipes off ev'ry tear.

In

Audin, per faltum refonat vox læta, propinquo

Sternite iter Domino : coràm quem quæritis, adftat

Ecce Deus. Deus, ille Deus cava culmina circùm,

Auritæque fonant rupes, fylvæque loquaces.

Afpice, devexo labentem ex æthere tellus

Excipit in gremium : prono fubfidite, montes,

Vertice; Numen adeft, humiles affurgite valles.

Afpera jam plano venienti tramite mollem

Pandite, faxa, viam; frondes jam fpargite, fylvæ,

Blandaque pacatis decurrite, flumina, ripis.

Huc, furdi, huc aures, oculos huc vertite, cæci :

Hic Vir hic eft, vobis patrum promiffus ab ævo.

Hic omnem ex oculis, infufo lumine, noctem

Eripiet, folemque dabit cælumque tueri.

Hic aurem obftructam fuperâ virtute recludet,

Mulcebitque novo cantu, numerifque fonoris.

Dulcè canet mutus, perniceque jam pede claudus

Exultim ludet, ceu faltans per juga cervus.

Jam dolor, et lachrymæ, et mœfto'queremonia vultu

Abfiftent terris : jam centum vincta catenis

T 2   Mors

In adamantine chains shall death be bound,

And hell's grim tyrant feel th' eternal wound.

  As the good shepherd tends his fleecy care,

Seeks freshest pasture and the purest air,

Explores the lost, the wand'ring sheep directs,

By day o'erfees them, and by night protects,

The tender lambs he raises in his arms,

Feeds from his hand, and in his bosom warms:

Thus shall mankind his guardian care engage,

The promised Father of the future age.

No more shall nation against nation rise,

Nor ardent warriors meet with hateful eyes,

Nor fields with gleaming steel be cover'd o'er,

The brazen trumpet kindle rage no more.

But useless lances into scythes shall bend,

And the broad faulchion in a ploughshare end.

Then palaces shall rise: the joyful son

Shall finish what his short-lived sire begun.

                      Their

Mors inferna ruet : capiti jam vulnus adactum
Sentiet æternâ Stygius sub nocte tyrannus.

Ac veluti paftor, cui dulcia ovilia curæ,
Pafcua læta gregi explorat zephyrofque falubres,
Noctes atque dies animis vigilantibus inftat,
Seu regit errantem, feu fortè per avia lapfam
Quærit ovem ; cafus omnes à matribus arcet ;
Ipfe levans ulnis teneros complectitur agnos,
Ipfe manu pafcit, fotofque in pectore mulcet :
Talis erit, tali populos pietate regendos
Sufcipiet fæcli cuftofque paterque futuri.
Tum placidâ gentes coalefcent pace, nec ultrà
In pugnas ftragemque ruent : rutilantia ferro
Agmina nec fternent adeò formidine terras,
Nec tuba terrifico martem ciet ærea cantu.
Sed priùs apta neci in falcem conflabitur hafta,
Inque ufum gravidi curvabitur enfis aratri.
Regia marmoreis furgent tum tecta columnis,
Exultanfque hæres rapti molimina patris

Ardua

'Their vines a shadow to their race shall yield,

And the same hand that sow'd, shall reap the field:

The swain in barren deserts with surprise

See lilies spring, and sudden verdure rise,

And start amidst the thirsty wilds to hear

New falls of water murm'ring in his ear.

On rifted rocks, the dragon's late abodes,

The green reed trembles, and the bulrush nods.

Waste, sandy vallies, once perplex'd with thorn,

The spiry fir and shapely box adorn.

To leafless shrubs the flow'ry palms succeed,

And od'rous myrtle to the noisome weed.

The lambs with wolves shall graze the verdant mead,

And boys in flow'ry bands the tiger lead.

The steer and lion at one crib shall meet,

And harmless serpents lick the pilgrim's feet.

The smiling infant in his hand shall take

The crested basilisk and speckled snake,

Pleased the green lustre of the scales survey,

And with their forky tongue shall innocently play.

Rise,

Ardua perficiet ; fibi quos confeverit agros,

Ipfe metet ; facient vineta nepotibus umbram.

Surgere tum cernet vafta inter rura colonus

Liliaque et lætos inopino gramine campos :

Audiet et trepidus fitientes inter arenas

Infolitum erumpens murmur fluctufque cadentes.

In fcopulo, nuper quà confedêre dracones,

Jam virides junci formofaque nutat arundo.

Quà deferta priùs vallis ftetit horrida dumis,

Confurgent abies crifpoque cacumine buxus :

Quà frutices nudi et fpinis paliurus amaris,

Floriferæ palmæ et myrti nafcentur odoræ.

Florea vincla puer tigri fubnectet inermi,

Permixtique lupis pafcent in montibus agni.

Cum tauro in ftabulis placidus leo ftabit apertis,

Ruricolæque pedes innoxia vipera lambet.

Criftatum bafilifcum infans viridemque colubrum

Excipiet plaudetque manu : fulgentia fquamis

Tergora luftrabit rifu, ludenfque trifulcæ

Spicula nec linguæ metuet nec inane venenum.

Regia

Rife, crown'd with light, imperial Salem, rife,

Exalt thy tow'ry head, and lift thy eyes.

See a long race thy fpacious courts adorn,

See future fons, and daughters yet unborn,

In crowding ranks on ev'ry fide they rife,

Demanding life, impatient for the fkies.

See barb'rous nations at thy gates attend,

Walk in thy light, and in thy temple bend.

See thy bright altars throng'd with proftrate kings,

And heap'd with produčts of Sabean fprings.

For thee Idume's fpicy forefts blow,

And feeds of gold in Ophir's mountains glow.

See heav'n its fparkling portals wide difplay,

And break upon thee in a flood of day.

No more the rifing fun fhall gild the morn,

Nor ev'ning Cynthia fill her filver horn :

But loft, diffolved in thy fuperior rays,

One tide of glory, one unclouded blaze

O'erflow

Regia surge Salem : radiis redimita corufcis
Surge, et turritum celfo caput infere cœlo.
Afpice, quanta tibi fpatiofa per atria lucet
Progenies : fuperas ardent evadere in auras
Et nati natæque, et qui nafcentur ab illis.
En tibi, fplendentis cœli nova figna fecutæ,
Barbaricæ agglomerant gentes : en ad tua læti
Limina contendunt gazis orientis onufti
Suppliciter reges, et natum Numen adorant.
Suavibus in fylvis tibi balfama gignit Idume,
Servat Ophir fulvis nutritum in montibus aurum.

Sed viden, interior latè tibi panditur aula
Cœlicolûm, totufque oculis illucet olympus.
Non jam mane novo Sol proferet ampliùs orbem,
Nec vefpertinum replebit Cynthia cornu :
Sed radiis immerfa tuis fua fidus utrumque
Lumina fubducet.   Noƈturnæ nefcius umbræ
Atria inextinƈtis tua veftiet ignibus æther.

T 5   Lucis

O'erflow thy courts.   The Light himſelf ſhall ſhine

Revealed, and God's eternal day be thine.

The ſeas ſhall waſte, the ſkies in ſmoke decay,

Rocks fall to duſt, and mountains melt away;

But fix'd his word, his ſaving pow'r remains,

Thy realm for ever laſts, thy own Messiah reigns.

Lucis origo, tuas penitus diffufa per arces,

Æternùm Deus ipfe fuo te numine complet.

Æquora inarefcent, rupes cum montibus altis

Flamma feret, fugient cœli ceu fumus in auras :

Aft hominum ftat fixa falus, ftat fœdere pacto

Lex, fummo jurata Deo : tibi regna, tuoque

Semper honos CHRISTO, fceptrumque decufque

    manebunt.

================

S. CATHARINA de Morte Triumphans.

ECLOGA.

THYRSIS, DAMON.

———————

CHRISTIADÆ flebant Catharin crudelia paſſam

Funera; vos, coryli, teſtes & littora Nili.

Quæ latebræ, aut qui vos ſaltus tenuêre, puellæ

Niliades, ſævâ Catharis cùm morte periret?

Nam neque Pyramidum ſacra culmina, nam neque

   pinguis

Ulla moram vobis faciebant rura Canopi.

O, cui *Belgarum Regina Auguſta per urbes

Credidit Auſtriacas rerum tractanda ſuarum

* Theſe two Eclogues in the firſt edition were dedicated to the late Count Cobenzl, Imperial Miniſter at the Court of Bruſſels.

Pondera,

Pondera, ſi qua tibi, curis aliquando remiſſis,

Hora vacat, nec te totum ſibi publica poſcunt

Munia, nos noſtramque, tua eſt, Clariſſime; Muſam

Aſpice, quamque ſuo defert ſtudioſa Patrono,

Hanc inter meritas hederam ſine ſerpere palmas.

Jam ſurgens Aurora polo dimoverat umbras,

Solque pruinoſos infuſo lumine montes

Sparſerat; extemplò curis vigilantibus acti,

E ſeptis miſêre greges ad paſcua Thyrſis,

Atque bonus Damon; extinctæ Virginis ambo

Ægri luctu, ambo calamos inflare periti.

Dum ſparſim tondent ſimæ virgulta capellæ,

Dum querulis agni ripam balatibus implent,

Hi procul à gregibus, neque enim conſiſtere mentem

Mœſta ſinit pietas, ſylvæ populantur honores,

Pallentes hederas & funereas cypariſſos,

Extremum tumulo munus. Poſtquam ardua montis

Et ſanctum tetigêre jugum, procumbit uterque

Pronus humi, nudoque gemens fert oſcula buſto.

Thyrſis

Thyrſis inexpletùm lacrymans, ſolatia luctûs

Nulla capit.   Via jam voci ut laxata dolore eſt,

Hæc ſecum gemitu & ſtudio jactabat inani.

Funde graves mecum, mea tibia, funde querelas.

Occidit heu! Catharis, Pharii lux maxima ruris

Occidit, immiti Catharis data victima letho.

Te juga, te valles, te noſtra mapalia, Virgo,

Ingemuêre : ipſi, nam te ſenſêre cadentem,

Balantes flevêre greges, luctuſque dedêre.

Te quoque Pyramides, te regia tecta, columnæ,

Et Pharos, & mœſti fleverunt ſaxa Canopi.

Funde graves mecum, mea tibia, funde querelas.

Cùm Catharis ſtudiis cœleſtibus incita colles

Per noſtros calamo Divos cantaret agreſti,

Pulſatæ numeros retulêre ad ſidera valles,

Auritæque cavis faliêre in montibus orni.

Jam vidui montes, valleſque ſilentia ſervant,

·Ni lugubrè gemens per littora murmuret Auſter.

Funde

Funde graves mecum, mea tibia, funde querelas.

Illa rudes animos cultu formavit agreſtûm,

Accenditque ſacro vitæ venientis amore.

Illa, nihil mortale canens, arguta Sophorum

Arma domat, victrixque ferocia ſubdere cogit

Colla Deo : ſed non ideo crudelia fata

Flectere, vel furias potuit mollire tyranni.

Funde graves mecum, mea tibia, funde querelas.

Hei mihi ! quid, Virgo, jam poſt túa funera ſperem ?

Certum eſt in tenebris inter deſerta locorum

Condere velle caput, dulceſque relinquere cœtus

Paſtorum, & mœſtis conſumere fletibus ævum.

Ibo, & quæ memori ſub pectore fixa reſervo,

Carmina per montes ſylvis meditabor & auris.

Hæc tanquam inſani mihi ſint medicina doloris !

Jam neque ſeceſſus nemorum, neque carmina nobis

Ipſa placent : rurſum virides concedite ſylvæ.

Protinus, infandi quando ſolatia caſûs

Reſtant nulla ſuper, ſævo ferienda tyranno

Colla

Colla dabo. Tecum pariter fic rumpere lucem,
Virgo, juvat, pulchramque pati per vulnera mortem.

Sifte graves mecum, mea tibia, fifte querelas.
Hæc Thyrfis, cui fic refpondit in ordine Damon.
Niliacæ Nymphæ, quis tum vos fenfus habebat,
Cùm Catharis flammas inter dentefque rotarum
Pendebat diftricta, & non muliebriter audens
Collectas tortorum iras, omnefque minantis
Una laceffebat gladios ignefque tyranni?

Tollite humo Catharim, fuper æthera tollite, Divi.
Cùm deprenfa manus inter jam ftaret, & ultro
Vitam, juffa mori, lictoris fubderet enfi,
Sanguineum facinus mucro horruit, atque pudicam
Vulnere cervicem timuit fignare cruento.
Quà niveis avulfum humeris caput excidit, albo
Lactea prorumpit falienti flumine lympha.

                                    Tollite

Tollite humo Catharim, fuper æthera tollite, Divi.

Quale nitent inter lactentia lilia mixtæ

Purpureo fplendore rofæ ; fublimè per auras

Qualis aquam juxta myrtus fe tollit, & omnem

Ambrofio fpirans fylvam perfundit odore ;

Aut Libani qualis ftat celfo in vertice cedrus,

Sic Pharias inter Catharis pulcherrima Nymphas.

Tollite humo Catharim, fuper æthera tollite, Divi.

India diffufo fpatiantem flumine Gangem

Sufpicit, Euphratem Babylon, & Parthia Tigrim :

Dum Catharis formofa fuum tenet incola Nilum,

Parthiaque, & Babylon concedet, & India Nilo.

Tollite humo Catharim, fuper æthera tollite, Divi.

Cùm diverfa ruens feptena per oftia Nilus

Divite fœcundat vicinos gurgite campos,

Vernat ager, vernant meffes, annique labores.

Sic ubi doctrinæ Catharis miracula promit,

Et liquidas recludit opes, fontefque falubres

Eloquii

Eloquii, læto virtus.se germine fundit,

Et felices cœlo animas plaudente reponit.

Tollite humo Catharim, super æthera tollite, Divi.

Attonitas audin' clangor quis perculit aures ?

Cœlicolûm pennata phalanx per nubila vectat

Virginis exuvias, famulisque exercitus alis

Plaudit ovans, notoque infert sacra offa sepulchro.

Tollite humo Catharim, super æthera tollite, Divi.

Salve fancte Sinai, mons ô gratissime cœlo,

Ante alios falve tanto dignate trophæo :

Tu face nimbosâ & præsentis numinis olim

Fulmine terrificus, prono nunc culmine mitis

Extinctos cineres, ductamque ex ordine pompam

Excipis, & gremio depostam amplecteris urnam.

Tollite humo Catharim, super æthera tollite, Divi.

Sed viden' æthereos Catharis superevolat orbes ;

Supra Euri Zephyrique domos, stellasque micantes

                                        Surgit,

Surgit, & æternum, jam cœli afcripta beatis
Diva choris, victâ ducit de morte triumphum.

Parcite, jam Catharis tenet æthera, parcite Divi.

S. CATHARINA.

S. CATHARINA de Philofophis Triumphans.

ECLOGA.

DICITE, Niliades, nam vos meminiffe poteftis,
Dicite, quæ Cathari quondam memorante, beata
Audiit Ægyptus, populofque edifcere juffit.

Sæpiùs illa feros fpe palmæ luferat hoftes,
Exueratque dolos cæcos, artefque tyranni.
Ille adeò indignans, innecti vincula captæ
In caveamque trahi mandat, circumque Lycæi.
Convenêre, quibus facundæ copia linguæ,
Aut mens acris erat.   Veniunt arguta dicacis
Agmina Ariftotelis ; tumidis Academica buccis
Turba venit ; venit & dubiis gens nata ferendis
                                    Sceptica ;

Sceptica; tum fufis rugofa per ora capillis
Horrentes Cynici, atque Epicuri exercitus omnis.

Jamque dies prædicta aderat, jam docta theatrum
Agmina complêrant, queis fe Maxentius infert
Spectator pugnæ.   Jam curva fedilia circùm
Infufum excipiunt populum, turbamque fonantem.
Stat fola in medio Catharis, velut alma rapaces
Agna lupos inter, tam forti pectore conftans,
Quàm rofeis formofa genis : fimul omnibus infit.
Tum verò arrectos narrantis ab ore videres
Socraticos pendere greges, tum nefcia flecti
Antehac, paulatim mollefcere corda tyrannum;
Non fic mirata eft Mofen Carmelia rupes,
Non fic Jeffiaden Solymæ ftupuêre canentem.

Namque canebat, uti vaftum per inane coactus
Numinis imperio, primùm concrevenit orbis
Ex nihilo, hic pulcher rerum, quem cernimus, ordo.
Vis æterna Dei, molem diffufa per omnem,

                                   Numine

Numine cuncta movet : præfens terramque polumque
Ille replet, totumque unus regit arbiter orbem.
Hinc ventis agitata tument, hinc ftrata quiefcunt
Æquora; fidereis hinc pafcitur ignibus æther.
Hinc fylvis autumnus opes, hinc gramina tellus
Verna parit, fegetefque novis cum fructibus æftas.

Inde genus mortale refert, Edenaque Tempe
Fatiferique efum pomi, pœnafque Parentum.
Ipfa ut deinde Dei, numen de numine, proles
Par Patri æterno, mortales fumpferit artus
Factus homo.—Ut, poftquam decreti temporis orbem
Vivendo explêrat, ligno moribundus ab alto,
Innocuo fontem reparârit fanguine mundum.
Illum expirantem, fufpiriaque ægra trahentem
Fleverunt elementa ; gravi conterrita motu
Terra tremit, mœftam templo cortina ruinam
Fiffa trahit, lacrymant aræ, tumulique dehifcunt.
Ipfum etiam, obducto nigrâ ferrugine vultu,
Officii puduit, patienti Numine, folem,

                                            Confciaque

Confciaque æternam pavit gens impia noctem.

At Chriftum, edomiti fpoliis Acherontis ovantem,

Tertia lux fuperas redivivum eduxit in auras,

Immortale, ingens, & non violabile numen.

Inde quater decies cùm fol reparaverat ortus,

Atque diem toties pronà nox clauferat umbrâ,

Ille triumphali victor jam lætus honore,

Patris in amplexus fublimè per aëra magnum

Ibat ovans, rerumque tenet per fæcula habenas,

Non magno Genitore minor; cui maxima mundi

Sidera torquenti manet inconcuffa poteftas.

His adjungit, uti noftræ memor ufque falutis,

Bis fenos, genus indoctum, fed vivida cœlo

Pectora, fanctorum comitum felegerit omni

Ex numero heroas, fua qui præcepta fecuti

Informes hominum mores, atque afpera cultu

Ingenia excolerent, legefque & facra docerent

Chrifticolûm.—At fi vera cano, fi magna rependo,

Vos

Vos quoque ne pudeat fubmittere dura vocanti
Corda Deo, tenebrifque oculos aperire fugatis.

Talia perftabat memorans & fixa manebat.
Attonitis ftat turba animis fufpenfa, nec audet
Hifcere quid contrà ; donec jam numinis ipfo
Impulfu trepidi rabiem fenfufque profanos
Excutiunt, unumque Deum unâ voce fatentur
Artificem mundi, cœlique crebique potentem.

FINIS

www.ingramcontent.com/pod-product-compliance
Lightning Source LLC
Chambersburg PA
CBHW032258280326

41932CB00009B/607